# PROMOTING EQUITY AND JUSTICE THROUGH PEDAGOGICAL PARTNERSHIP

# SERIES ON **ENGAGED LEARNING** AND **TEACHING**

Series Editors: Jessie L. Moore and Peter Felten

*Mind the Gap*
*Global Learning at Home and Abroad*
Edited by Nina Namaste and Amanda Sturgill, with Neal W. Sobania and Michael Vande Berg

*Promoting Equity and Justice Through Pedagogical Partnership*
By Alise de Bie, Elizabeth Marquis, Alison Cook-Sather, and Leslie Patricia Luqueño

*Key Practices for Fostering Engaged Learning*
*A Guide for Faculty and Staff*
By Jessie L. Moore

*The Faculty Factor*
*Developing Faculty Engagement With Living Learning Communities*
Edited by Jennifer Eidum and Lara Lomicka

# PROMOTING EQUITY AND JUSTICE THROUGH PEDAGOGICAL PARTNERSHIP

*Alise de Bie, Elizabeth Marquis,*

*Alison Cook-Sather, and*

*Leslie Patricia Luqueño*

*Foreword by Alexis Giron*

*Series Foreword by Jessie L. Moore and Peter Felten*

**Series on Engaged Learning and Teaching**

Copublished in association with

STERLING, VIRGINIA

Published by Stylus Publishing, LLC.
22883 Quicksilver Drive
Sterling, Virginia 20166-2019

Library of Congress Cataloging-in-Publication Data
Names: De Bie, Alise, author. | Marquis, Elizabeth, author. | Cook-Sather, Alison,
   1964- author. | Luqueño, Leslie Patricia, author.
Title: Promoting equity and justice through pedagogical partnership / Alise de Bie,
   Elizabeth Marquis, Alison Cook-Sather, and Leslie Patricia Luqueño ; foreword by
   Alexis Giron.
Description: First edition. | Sterling, Virginia: Stylus Publishing, LLC., 2021. | Series:
   Engaged learning and teaching | Includes bibliographical references and index. |
   Summary: "This book contributes to the literature on pedagogical partnership and
   equity in education by integrating theory, synthesizing research, and providing
   concrete examples of the ways partnership can contribute to more equitable
   educational systems"-- Provided by publisher.
Identifiers: LCCN 2021017921 (print) | LCCN 2021017922 (ebook) | ISBN
   9781642672084 (cloth) | ISBN 9781642672091 (paperback) | ISBN
   9781642672107 (adobe pdf) | ISBN 9781642672114 (epub)
Subjects: LCSH: Professional learning communities. | College teaching. | People
   with social disabilities--Education (Higher) | Educational equalization. | Student
   participation in administration. | Student participation in curriculum planning. |
   Critical pedagogy.
Classification: LCC LB2331 .D39 2021  (print) | LCC LB2331  (ebook) | DDC
   378.1/25--dc23
LC record available at https://lccn.loc.gov/2021017921
LC ebook record available at https://lccn.loc.gov/2021017922

13-digit ISBN: 978-1-64267-208-4 (cloth)
13-digit ISBN: 978-1-64267-209-1 (paperback)
13-digit ISBN: 978-1-64267-210-7 (library networkable e-edition)
13-digit ISBN: 978-1-64267-211-4 (consumer e-edition)

Printed in the United States of America

All first editions printed on acid-free paper
that meets the American National Standards Institute
Z39-48 Standard.

Bulk Purchases

Quantity discounts are available for use in workshops and
for staff development.

Call 1-800-232-0223

First Edition, 2021

*To all the partners who have worked, are working,*
*or will work toward equity and justice.*

# CONTENTS

*P*romoting Equity and Justice Through Pedagogical Partnership is part of the Series on Engaged Learning and Teaching, published by Stylus in partnership with the Center for Engaged Learning at Elon University. The series is designed for a multidisciplinary audience of higher education faculty, staff, graduate students, educational developers, administrators, and policymakers interested in research-informed engaged learning practices. Although individual books in the series might most appeal to those interested in a specific topic, each volume concisely synthesizes research for nonexperts and addresses the broader implications of this particular work for higher education, including effective practices for teaching, curriculum design, and educational policies. All books in the series are supplemented by open-access resources hosted on the Center for Engaged Learning's website.

*Promoting Equity and Justice Through Pedagogical Partnership* serves as an excellent example of our goals for this book series. The book's critical analysis of partnership, rich case studies, and thoughtful attention to equity will equip readers to enact just practices in their classrooms and programs. This book challenges readers to understand and redress the harms that many students experience in higher education, even in student-centered practices like pedagogical partnerships. As the authors demonstrate, that difficult work is necessary to promote equity and justice in and through engaged learning. Supplemental resources for *Promoting Equity and Justice Through Pedagogical Partnership*—including additional examples, discussion questions for reading groups, video interviews with leading scholars, and more—are available at https://www.centerforengagedlearning.org/books/promoting-equity-and-justice-through-pedagogical-partnership/.

We are grateful to Alise de Bie, Elizabeth Marquis, Alison Cook-Sather, and Leslie Patricia Luqueño for contributing this significant text to the series. Their research and practical strategies will positively inform readers' partnerships and their efforts to promote equity and justice on their campuses.

To learn more about the Series on Engaged Learning and Teaching, including how to propose a book, please visit https://www.centerforengagedlearning.org/publications/.

Series Editors, Jessie L. Moore and Peter Felten
Center for Engaged Learning, Elon University

When I was growing up, I never understood why it was so important that I finish high school; I just knew that I wanted it to be something I achieved. I come from a family of six older siblings, and only one of them completed high school before me. She maintained her life in New York, while we made a living of ours in Houston, Texas.

It was always a dream of mine to attend college, where I could separate enough to get to experience and advocate for myself, but still be able to continue to support my family. Postsecondary education would mean that I would be able to end this generational poverty that seemed to have gotten us stuck in a life of federal assistance and constant movement. I loved learning, and I loved school, so this was the place for me. I received a full-tuition scholarship to attend Bryn Mawr College, where my true success would soon begin.

Coming into Bryn Mawr, I was aware of the lack of diversity, but it was consistently counterpointed with statements such as, "At least it's more diverse than other places." There was also the idea of women's empowerment, more women in STEM, a great deal of support, and so much more that came with attending a traditional all-women's institution. Despite the potential of all these ideals and supports, my first semester at Bryn Mawr was one of my toughest semesters. I quickly began to realize that many parts of my identity contributed to my sense of nonbelonging in academia and insecurities in the classroom. A low-income, first-generation Afro-Latina from a single-parent household had been thrown into a predominantly White institution, taking premed classes with predominantly White students and predominantly White professors. It seemed as though my sciences in high school were not taught to the degree that many others seemed to obtain; unlike my classmates, I had never been exposed to a laboratory setting.

I consistently told myself, "We did not all start in the same spot; some students began with an advantage." And although I reminded myself of this when I was struggling, I didn't seem to believe it. I was afraid of reaching out to professors. I was afraid of speaking up in class. I couldn't ask my classmates to tutor me; they'd think I was dumb. I'd just be one of the "brown girls" that didn't understand. I went through the first 3 years of my undergraduate career with this mindset. That was until I became a student consultant for the Students as Learners and Teachers (SaLT) program at Bryn Mawr and Haverford Colleges. Since the first day in that role, I knew that this position would impact my life, but I was not aware of how much and how fast it would actually do so.

I had taken up multiple roles on campus in my first 3 years, including admissions tour guide, treasurer and eventually president of the Mujeres Latinx group, student leader of conversations about race, dining hall supervisor, coordinator and a member of the payroll team, and a mentor for the college's first-year THRIVE program. All of these roles offered me chances to throw myself into my community and build my résumé, and they also seemed like a way to build my confidence and replace the lack of self-esteem I experienced in the classroom. But they didn't quite do that. Being a student consultant was different.

These positions brought me opportunities to fight for social change and also defend and protect against discrimination. They gave me the opportunity to stand up for the future generations of low-income, first-generation Black and Latinx women who would enter spaces similar to the ones I've sat in. They helped me advocate for myself and others in every other aspect of my life but the classroom. I could never quite seem to make those same changes in my academic spaces. Everywhere else, I knew I was advocating for more than just myself; I was doing it for my people and for my ancestors. Like Elizabeth Acevedo's (n.d.) poem "Afro-Latina" beautifully describes, I am *"el destino de mi gente"* (the destiny of my people). I thought that if I could see myself making changes in my community, they, and I, would forget that I was struggling to make them proud in my academics.

When I stepped inside a classroom, where I would be judged and graded, it all felt exposing, vulnerable. Everything I'd ever done in my other life-changing positions, for these exact moments, disappeared, and I was left alone and silent; until I became a student consultant. Of course, I had heard it all before: It was not my fault that I was struggling; *higher* education is inaccessible. But how could *I* not blame myself for being unable to strive in class? Little did I know, this is where I would learn that those fights for social change can also be made in the classroom, where I understood that academic spaces were not designed for people like me.

As a student consultant, I am given the opportunity to sit face to face with a faculty member who volunteers to receive feedback on what seems to be working well in their classroom and on what they might do to become a better educator. I am able to put myself, a student with multiple underrepresented identities, into an academic space where I am not only being heard as a student but as a partner as well. This was my chance to make up for all of the struggles left unsaid, my chance to make it up to myself for not being the advocate I told myself I would be. However, in a sense, I felt like a hypocrite; I felt like an imposter. For 3 years, I had remained silent as White students took up space in the classroom and in office hours, while I continued to get intimidated by professors who encouraged me *not* to remain in some courses or questioned whether I belonged in the field. But I knew that in order to make up for it all, I had to use my voice in this position to speak up for the next generation of students with underrepresented identities in higher education. Most importantly, I had to use my voice to help myself heal from all of the trauma that these classrooms caused me and my self-esteem, and the harm that I caused myself by not being my one, true advocate.

My main focus as a student consultant was to target how race, ethnicity, and educational background may affect inclusivity and comfortability in a STEM-based classroom. I focused on demographics like race and ethnicity, types of schools that students attended, and their comfort in discussions. In my role, I was able to become a part of a group of students who strived to make a difference in the classroom. Because we are given the opportunity to observe a professor's class once a week, we put ourselves in their classroom as an extra set of eyes and an extra voice. Instead of focusing on the material, we are able to spend our energy on the way it is presented to the students enrolled in the course. This position includes weekly meetings with other student consultants who may be experiencing similar ideas and issues in their classrooms, and these student consultants also bring up completely different ideas that spark different conversations.

In addition to the weekly student discussions, I met weekly with my faculty partner. We clicked automatically. I had expected to want to tear a White, cis-heterosexual male to shreds for his pedagogical practices. My faculty partner did not give me that chance, and I'm glad for so many reasons. It was actually a relief to work with someone who understood me as a partner, a student, and as a person. I was able to use ways that I have struggled in my courses, specifically STEM courses, to bring awareness to those potential characteristics in a group of students and emphasize the use of other teaching strategies. This partnership also allowed me to assist in the design of a course in a way that I, as a struggling student, might have felt more involved in the lesson.

One word I would use to describe this program is *healing.* I was given the opportunity to heal from all the harm that higher education and educators have caused. I was given a second chance—I was able to go back in time and reflect on things I wish I had known when I was sitting in those undergraduate desks during my first 3 years. I participated in the SaLT program to advocate for myself and for other students of multiple underrepresented identities who were not taught to speak up for themselves and who were not given the privilege of being informed that we are allowed to take up space; we are allowed to ask for help; we are allowed and entitled to ask for extensions and office hours and assistance. None of those things make us weak.

Writing the foreword for this book gives me another opportunity to heal from that sense of not belonging and to make my voice heard. This book is important because it brings awareness to educators all over about the harm they might be doing to students. Though much of this harm may not be intentional, the impact that it has on these students is great, from instilling embarrassment for attending office hours to discouraging them from majoring in a certain field. This book does a great job of articulating my experiences in a way that I cannot find a way to do. From its description of epistemic (knowledge-related), affective (feeling-related), and ontological (being-related) violence and harm to its strong advocacy for equity and inclusion, this book has helped me validate the challenges that I have faced in an academic and professional setting.

This book will also validate the experiences of other students who have suffered from epistemic, affective, and ontological harms in postsecondary education. They will see their stories in its pages, just like I saw mine, and they will feel affirmed, and they will see that they are not alone. The book also offers educators a way of thinking about and naming the harms students experience; it gives them a framework for how to act on them, not just perceive them. If we don't name these things the way this book does, in maybe strong but very accurate terms, then we can't work as actively against those things, and they will keep happening. Through the partnership work I experienced and that is described in this book, I healed from much of the harm I experienced and also saw how the work can help others heal. I hope people will read this book thinking about both the harm that has been done and the healing that can be done.

Alexis Giron
Bryn Mawr College, Class of 2020

# AN INVITATION TO PROMOTE EQUITY AND JUSTICE THROUGH PARTNERSHIP

Reflecting on a semester-long partnership with a faculty member focused on creating more equitable learning experiences, an undergraduate student described why she chose to engage in this work:

> I had always had an interest in learning about how people learn, especially since I have come from a really underserved educational background myself. I learned very quickly at Bryn Mawr [College] that I didn't necessarily have all the resources that I absolutely needed to be able to thrive automatically. As I started thinking about that more, I realized that so much of the onus when I was in high school really was on my teachers proactively redressing some habits they might have had to accommodate a person like me, and I began to think about ways in which I could help professors become more wakeful to the needs of that structural disadvantage as well. (Quoted in Cook-Sather 2018b, 928)

This reflection throws into relief the inequities that precede students' arrival on college and university campuses and that are perpetuated once they are there. The "structural disadvantage" this student names, we argue, is not simply a challenge but rather constitutes and is constituted by multiple forms of violence—epistemic (knowledge-related), affective (feelings-related), and ontological (being-related)—that do harm to students, as Alexis Giron also noted in her foreword. In this book we argue and show that pedagogical partnership can contribute to redressing these harms and promoting greater equity and justice.

That the university has been an exclusive and inequitable institution is a well-known reality for students (as well as for staff and faculty members) from equity-seeking groups traditionally underrepresented in postsecondary education. Although these groups (and the terms used to identify them) vary across country and institutional context, in the North American locations from which we write they include First Nations, Métis, and Inuit students; Black, Indigenous, people of color (BIPOC), and racialized students; first-generation college students; Two-Spirit, lesbian, gay, bisexual, transgender, and queer and questioning students (2SLGBTQ); low-income students; students from minority faith backgrounds; disabled students; and those identifying with mental health disabilities/madness or as Mad (see de Bie 2019b for further elaboration of this term). Although postsecondary education has, ostensibly, expanded from affording access only to the elite to providing universal access for the whole population (Trow 2007), a significant body of scholarship has demonstrated that barriers to access and systemic inequities continue to affect students from a wide range of marginalized groups in postsecondary education (Collins, Azmat, and Rentschler 2019; Daddow 2016; Devlin 2013; Doran et al. 2015; Harper 2019; Harper, Patton, and Wooden 2009; Marquis, Fudge Schormans et al. 2016; Marquis et al. 2012; Simmons et al. 2013).

This book presents a conceptual framework, case studies, reflections, and recommendations focused on how pedagogical partnership can redress the harms students from equity-seeking groups experience in postsecondary education. *Pedagogical partnership* is one of several terms that have emerged (e.g., *student–faculty partnership, students as partners*) to name approaches through which faculty, academic staff, and professional staff "engage students as co-learners, co-researchers, co-inquirers, co-developers, and co-designers" (Healey, Flint, and Harrington 2016, 2). We recognize that the term does not mean the same thing across contexts or to all people (Cook-Sather et al. 2018), but it is, currently, among the terms available for describing this work, the one most closely aligned with our commitment to equity and justice in postsecondary education. The collaborative processes of partnership through which students, faculty, and staff work together to shape their educational environment, practices, and outcomes (Bryson, Furlonger, and Rinaldo-Langridge 2015) are underpinned by the premises of respect, reciprocity, and shared responsibility (Cook-Sather, Bovill, and Felten 2014). Some scholars of partnership have recast these premises in "the more explicitly feminist terms of agency, accountability, and affinity" (Cates, Madigan, and Reitenauer 2018, 37). As all these terms suggest, partnership refers to "a collaborative, reciprocal process through which all participants have the opportunity to contribute equally, although not necessarily in the same ways, to curricular or pedagogical conceptualization, decision making, implementation, investigation, or analysis" (Cook-Sather, Bovill, and Felten 2014, 6–7).

In the conceptual model that Healey, Flint, and Harrington (2014, 2016) offered, there are four broad areas in which students might work in partnership with faculty and staff: (a) learning, teaching, and assessment; (b) subject-based research and inquiry; (c) scholarship of teaching and learning; and (d) curriculum design and pedagogic consultancy. These can, of course, overlap and inform one another, and often do. Each has potential to redress the harms students experience but none automatically does so. For example, as we discuss further in chapter 3, partnership in each of these areas invites students into processes of knowledge production and has the potential to recognize, affirm, and support students as knowers, thereby helping to redress the harm resulting from continually having one's knowledge as a student and a member of one or more equity-seeking groups discounted. Nevertheless, given that we all enter partnerships with prejudices and preconceptions shaped through our existence in dominant society, this affirmation of typically disqualified knowledge is not guaranteed. Although partnership itself might contribute to reducing prejudicial judgments about the knowledge of others by creating opportunities to work across difference, it can only do so if it is thoughtfully enacted. Only through intentional naming of inequities and injustices—violences—and resulting harms, through equally intentional structuring of opportunities that enact partnership principles, and through further revision of these steps, as we explore throughout this book, can pedagogical partnership realize its full potential to redress harms and promote equity and justice.

By arguing that inequity is an act of violence that leads to various forms of harm, we aim to highlight that how institutions structure disadvantage is not a neutral policy or practice. As we explain in chapter 2, we use the language of *violence* and *harm* to signal the severity of what students from equity-seeking groups traditionally underrepresented in postsecondary education often experience. Specifically, we use *violence* to name what is done (by institutions and individuals to preserve dominant structures and processes), *harm* to name what is experienced (by many students who belong to equity-seeking groups), and *injustice* to characterize the phenomenon that the two constitute together. Our commitment to using these terms builds on existing work on inequity but intentionally uses this stronger language (as others like Kendi [2019] have done, as we discuss further in chapter 2). Although faculty and staff also experience these violences and associated harms, our focus in this book is on students' experiences.

Given that many existing approaches to addressing inequities students experience as a result of structural disadvantage are problematic or otherwise lacking (Ahmed 2012; Gibson 2015; Smit 2012), there is a pressing need to explore and disseminate alternative means of working toward equity and justice within postsecondary education contexts. The conceptual framework we offer in chapter 2 names and analyzes the epistemic, affective, and ontological violence and resulting harms marginalized students experience. It also affords us an opportunity to reread (in chapter 3) the scholarship on pedagogical partnership in the terms the framework provides. Furthermore, it allows us to present (in chapter 4) case studies of and reflections on our own work through partnership that endeavor to redress these three interrelated forms of harm and to work toward greater equity and justice. Finally, the conceptual framework lets us imagine how partnership work done at the individual level can reinforce some injustices, if we are not careful, but also can help us begin to address these at the structural or institutional level (as we mention in chapter 3 and elaborate in chapter 5, as our examples in chapter 6 illustrate, and as our recommendations in chapter 7 propose).

## Who We Are

The four of us have been variously involved in the struggle for greater equity on campus—serving on equity-focused task forces, committees, and policy development groups; attending to social justice issues and approaches in our own formal and informal teaching; and conducting research on enhancing equity in education. Alise de Bie has also spent a decade organizing with Mad and disabled students to create alternative peer supports on campus, negotiate entitlements to accommodation, and demand widespread accessibility. Although being relatively new to this work, Elizabeth (Beth) Marquis has designed and supported educational development activities connected to accessibility and inclusion. Alison Cook-Sather has spent over 25 years working with students to launch campus-wide social justice initiatives; facilitating faculty pedagogy seminars focused on diversity, equity, and inclusion; and directing an academic minor focused on related work. Leslie Patricia Luqueño has contributed as a student partner to a variety of pedagogical endeavors such as participating in the SaLT program, holding a student representative role on Haverford College's committee for educational policy, and working alongside Alison as a research partner. We have found ways to understand and take up issues of equity across a range of disciplinary backgrounds, including Mad(ness) studies; disability studies; gender studies and feminist research; social work; theater and film studies; educational studies; scholarship of teaching and learning; political science; anthropology; and Latin American, Iberian, and Latinx studies. In short, we have adopted, used, pushed, exploited, and tinkered with the formalized channels available to us for making change on campus—and we have found them insufficient to redress the injustices and harms of postsecondary education. Some of us have also participated in institutionally unsanctioned strategies. These too have their place, and their costs.

We have also all worked in pedagogical partnership, both through formal partnership programs in our institutions and in more informal venues. Within these partnerships, we have observed and experienced the potential for partnership-based ways of working across institutional roles to envision and realize greater equity for students from equity-seeking groups who take part, and for wider changes in teaching practice and campus climates. Although a growing number of publications (e.g., Colón García 2017; Cook-Sather 2018b; Cook-Sather, Des-Ogugua, and Bahti 2018; de Bie et al. 2019; Marquis et al. forthcoming; Perez 2016; Reyes and Adams 2017) have begun to explore the relationships between partnership and equity and inclusion, demonstrating that partnership has the potential to contribute to more just and equitable institutions, this topic still requires further inquiry and theorization. No resource has yet been produced that synthesizes the range of existing findings on partnership and equity, offers a careful analysis of these in order to promote further research and inquiry, and draws on these processes to offer both examples and recommendations for practice. This absence is in keeping with the observation offered by Patton et al. (2019) that there is an overall lack of research on specific equity and justice initiatives implemented in postsecondary education contexts and, within the existing research, a lack of critical analysis of systems of oppression that "create the need for initiatives to be established in the first place" (192). This book seeks to amplify, extend, and contribute to these conversations.

## Context: Injustice in Postsecondary Education and Calls for Redress

Our work is situated in and builds on current and ongoing efforts to redress systemic injustices in postsecondary education. In the Canadian and U.S. contexts, national and local legislation applies in various ways to postsecondary education, resulting in institutional policies and practices focused on preventing and addressing discrimination and enhancing accessibility (Marquis, Fudge Schormans et al. 2016; Marquis et al. 2012). Beyond compliance obligations, institutions are also offering more expansive endorsement of equity and inclusion principles. For example, "Inclusive Excellence Principles" have been adopted by 96 universities across Canada (Bohanon 2018; Universities Canada 2017), and several Canadian institutions have signed on to the Dimensions Charter, an initiative piloted by the Canadian government, which is intended to foster "increased research excellence, innovation and creativity within the postsecondary sector across all disciplines, through greater equity, diversity and inclusion" (Government of Canada 2019). In the United States, the Association of American Colleges and Universities produced a report entitled "Toward a Model of Inclusive Excellence in Postsecondary Institutions" (Williams, Berger, and McClendon 2005) and, more recently, resources such as *From Equity Talk to Equity Walk: Expanding Practitioner Knowledge for Racial Justice in Higher Education* (McNair, Bensimon, and Malcolm-Piqueux 2020).

At the intersection of the global COVID-19 pandemic and the newly revealed extent of ongoing anti-Black racism that catalyzed in the summer of 2020 what may be the largest protest movement in U.S. history, we see institutions and individuals intensifying their focus on dismantling inequitable and unjust systems and practices. There is a more explicit naming of the violence that has been and continues to be suffered, and there is, as former president Barack Obama has argued, new hope in the diversity of people fighting to end injustice (Friedler 2020).

These sorts of aspirational commitments and newly forming uprisings are making their way into institutional policy and planning. In both the United States and Canada, colleges and universities are creating comprehensive campus-wide "Equity, Diversity, and Inclusion" strategies to improve equity on a number of fronts (Iverson 2007). These include a focus on areas such as student recruitment, programmatic support, research and scholarship, and institutional climate (Tamtik and Guenter 2019). Scholars have likewise noted the creation of formal structures on college and university campuses, such as offices of diversity and chief diversity officers to fill them (Kwak, Gavrila, and Ramirez 2019; Tamtik and Guenter 2019), and diversity committees at both institutional and departmental levels (Doyle and George 2008; George, Shera, and Tat Tsang 1998; MacDonald et al. 2003). Catalyzed by the intersection of the global COVID-19 pandemic and the uprisings, institutional leaders are posting antiracism statements and beginning to enact long-overdue changes in ways of thinking and being.

University–community engagement initiatives have been proliferating, with pipeline programs seeking to facilitate the entry into postsecondary education of underrepresented groups and new services focused on the retention and academic success of marginalized students (Balch 2019; Glauser 2018; Universities Canada n.d.). Researchers and advocates have called for the better collection of demographic data in order to more adequately track efforts to increase diversity and address persistent inequities and underrepresentation in postsecondary education contexts (McDonald and Ward 2017; Moriarty and Murray 2007). And finally, faculty development initiatives and scholarship are proposing, preparing, and facilitating training on enhancing inclusion in teaching and learning (Haynie 2018; Marquis, Jung et al. 2016; Padden and Ellis 2015; Queen's University 2019), some responding directly to changes in teaching and learning demanded by recent protests (e.g., Academics for Black Survival and Wellness 2020).

Despite these initiatives and evolving efforts, however, injustice persists. Legislation such as the Higher Education Act (HEA), adopted in the United States in 1965 and reauthorized in various forms since, has sought to expand access and opportunity and increase the numbers of underrepresented students in higher education, but it has not succeeded in ensuring access to all students (Gaston 2018). Moreover, achieving (more) "equitable access" does not necessarily correspond to ensuring "equitable outcomes"—calling attention to how gaining access to the university is not the same as accruing the same benefit from the university (Fletcher et al. 2013). A focus on legislative compliance often results in "bare-minimum" efforts, where the focus is on providing what one is "entitled" to (e.g., academic or workplace accommodations) rather than the fullness of what is actually needed, and a system driven by complaints and risk management instead of proactive and transformative change (LePeau, Hurtado, and Williams 2019). Policy-based approaches to enhancing equity, diversity, and inclusion have been widely critiqued; such approaches, like many initiatives that purport to enhance equity in postsecondary education, have often described underrepresented groups as deficient against a White, male, nondisabled norm, faulting individuals—rather than systemic factors—for poor performance and recommending the creation of programs and services to compensate and rehabilitate these deficits (Daddow 2016; Gibson 2015; Iverson 2007; Smit 2012; Thomas 2002). The "addition" of these new services for marginalized groups has often failed to address the root causes of oppression, with programming set up by and for students from equity-seeking groups routinely pegged as nonessential and underfunded, thus making it difficult to effect institutional change (Patton et al. 2019). It is in part this inadequacy that prompted widespread authoring of open letters written to the members of postsecondary education institutions in the spring and summer of 2020, yet again naming structural inequities and injustices in postsecondary education and demanding change, echoing similar calls that have been issued for decades.

Although new equity-focused appointments have been created in recent years and may proliferate in response to recent demands, this can "actually signal a cordoning off of commitment rather than an institutional goal of diversity" (Ahmed 2012, 23), contributing to an overall trend whereby "the origins of and systems that perpetuate discrimination are uninterrogated, and advantage remains camouflaged (Ladson-Billings and Tate, 1995)" (Iverson 2007, 598). What's more, "diversity" has often been framed as useful to advancing a university's reputation, resulting in the marketing of diverse bodies as commodified property (Iverson 2007). Patton et al. (2019) consequently have observed:

> Students engaged in the current era of protest would argue against notions of progress over the last 50 years as they continue to work collectively and strategize in hopes that their voices and perspectives will be acknowledged and addressed. Progress in the present context is, therefore, relative. (175)

Many of the words used to talk about "inclusion" have also been adopted as institutional rhetoric, while "actions to support these messages may not occur" (Hoffman and Mitchell 2016, 278). Following Stewart (2017), who has argued that "diversity and inclusion rhetoric asks fundamentally different questions and is concerned with fundamentally different issues than efforts seeking equity and justice," our work commits to equity and justice:

> Diversity asks, "Who's in the room?" Equity responds: "Who is trying to get in the room but can't? Whose presence in the room is under constant threat of erasure?"
>
> Inclusion asks, "Has everyone's ideas been heard?" Justice responds, "Whose ideas won't be taken as seriously because they aren't in the majority?" . . .
>
> Diversity celebrates increases in numbers that still reflect minoritized status on campus and incremental growth. Equity celebrates reductions in harm, revisions to abusive systems and increases in supports for people's life chances as reported by those who have been targeted. (para. 10)

It is within this larger context of discussions of (in)equity, (in)justice, inclusion, and diversity that we offer this book. We are concerned with the epistemic, affective, and ontological forms of violence that leave some students under threat of erasure and facing the harm that results from these forms of violence. We value the knowledge of students from equity-seeking groups that is disqualified and not taken seriously. We affirm and pursue reductions in harm, increases in support, and transformation of the systems that caused harm to occur. In an effort to act on these concerns, values, and affirmations, we present pedagogical partnership as one, although certainly not the only, approach to redressing harms and pursuing justice.

## This Book: Focus, Content, and Audience

Coauthored by a postdoctoral fellow (Alise), two faculty members (Beth and Alison), and an undergraduate student (Leslie), this book advances the *book's central claim* PROMOTING EQUITY AND JUSTICE THROUGH PART?

10

argument that pedagogical partnerships can and do contribute
and justice by redressing harms caused by epistemic, affective,
logical forms of violence endemic to postsecondary education. We
introducing and applying a conceptual framework that seeks to (a) recognize
forms of violence and resulting harms often left unattended (and aggravated)
by popular analyses and approaches to inclusion on campus, as well as by the
pedagogical partnership literature; (b) extend the existing literature on how
pedagogical partnerships contribute to equity by synthesizing it through a
focus on epistemic, affective, and ontological effects; and (c) deepen reflection on the tensions, limitations, unanswered questions, inspiration, and
hope this framework offers our ongoing work.

The conceptual framework advanced here takes inspiration from Alise's
doctoral research (de Bie 2019a) and prior work we have done together to
describe how partnerships address epistemic forms of harm and contribute
to supporting more equitable teaching practices (de Bie et al. 2019; Cook-
Sather et al. 2019; Marquis et al. forthcoming). It also draws on Leslie's work
to theorize epistemic violence (through grant-supported research into how
partnerships promote equity) and Alison's work on how partnership can foster culturally responsive practice (Cook-Sather and Agu 2013; Cook-Sather
and Des-Ogugua 2019) and respect and belonging for underrepresented students (Cook-Sather 2018b, 2020; Cook-Sather and Seay 2020). Finally, it
builds on Beth's contributions to scholarship exploring access to partnership
programs (Marquis, Jayaratnam et al. 2019; Marquis et al. 2018) and considering the relationships between partnership and social change (Guitman
and Marquis 2020).

Our argument for the potential of pedagogical partnership to redress
epistemic, affective, and ontological harms is also informed by our experiences designing, facilitating, and participating in equity-focused partnership
initiatives. These initiatives include a new equity stream of a pedagogical
partnership program at McMaster University (Marquis, Carrasco-Acosta
et al. 2019); the Students as Learners and Teachers (SaLT) pedagogical
partnership program at Bryn Mawr and Haverford Colleges (Cook-Sather
2018a, 2019, 2020) that focuses on inclusive and responsive classroom
practices; and the more recent institutional leveraging of SaLT in pursuit
of more equitable practices (Cook-Sather et al. 2020). We draw as well on
our different identities, experiences, and positions within postsecondary
education and our respective and shared analyses of harm and pedagogical
partnership.

Following this first chapter, the book is organized into six chapters, which
we have noted previously and which are intended to be read in sequence the
first time through.

Chapter 2 presents a conceptual framework for understanding epistemic, affective, and ontological violences and resulting harms that students from equity-seeking groups face in postsecondary education, and that are in need of redress. We develop this conceptual framework in conversation with quoted student experiences of such harms.

Chapter 3 then applies this conceptual framework to the pedagogical partnership literature, highlighting the ways in which partnership work may have pushed against epistemic, affective, and ontological harms from associated violence without naming it in these terms and the promise of partnership to contribute to redressing these harms to bring about greater equity and justice. We draw on student experiences quoted in published research that we and others have conducted, unpublished data from three ethics-board-approved studies (see Appendix A), and works in progress.

Chapter 4 grounds the conceptual framework and our rereading of partnership literature by offering two case studies of pedagogical partnership in practice. The first case study focuses on the pedagogical development and curriculum (re)design work Alison and Leslie have been involved in at Bryn Mawr and Haverford Colleges, where this work coexists with inquiry and more formal partnership research. The second case focuses on coinquiry in the scholarship of teaching and learning that Beth and Alise contribute to at McMaster University, where this work coexists with pedagogical- and curricular-focused partnership work. We apply the framework to these examples, parsing out associated epistemic, affective, and ontological impacts.

Chapter 5 explores the complexities surfaced by our framework, including the conditions under which partnerships themselves may risk reproducing epistemic, affective, or ontological harms, or prevent the realization of intended and possible epistemic, affective, and ontological redress. Applying the framework in this way allows us to reconsider tensions already well recognized in the partnership literature, such as challenges navigating power differentials in partnership, and brings to light other less known and discussed challenges that require our attention if partnership is to contribute to greater justice. It also offers space for us to imagine and propose strategies for mediating these possibilities so that partnerships are more likely to meaningfully address inequity.

Chapter 6 focuses on the future of pedagogical partnership and shares a perspective from each author on exciting and important new directions for inquiry and practice as we work in partnership with equity-focused intentions. It also poses questions to help readers consider how the framework might apply to diverse individual, institutional, and national contexts.

Chapter 7 summarizes the overarching themes developed through the book and leaves the reader with encouragement and a set of questions and recommendations for further inquiry and discussion.

We write for a diverse audience of faculty, students, staff, educational developers, diversity workers, and administrators in postsecondary education looking for new ways of thinking about and engaging in equity and justice work; seasoned and novice participants in partnership seeking to reflect on their practice, as well as those expanding their partnership work more fulsomely to consider issues of equity; members of equity-seeking groups whose experiences of institutional violence are often underrecognized and who are developing and seeking strategies for redressing the harms that result from such violence; our colleagues engaged in related kinds of partnership work (e.g., community–university partnerships; service users partnering with service providers; partnerships across identity or issue-based groups) who face and contribute insight into similar complexities; and postsecondary education researchers investigating (in)equity at their institutions.

In applying the new conceptual framework we present, we are intentional in using our own programmatic examples and drawing on our personal perspectives in an effort to recognize our own situatedness and not to claim to speak for those in other contexts. We recognize the concerns that much partnership literature has come from and spoken to English-speaking, "Western" contexts (Bindra et al. 2018; Kaur, Awang-Hashim, and Kaur 2018; Pounder, Ho Hung-lam, and Groves 2016) and thus emphasize that the case studies we offer are not intended to serve as universally applicable exemplars, but rather as one set of possibilities that resonate with our own experiences and institutional locations. We invite others to take up this work, revise and apply it as appropriate to their contexts, and in so doing perhaps to develop revisions and extensions of it.

Moreover, while our focus here is on students, we also acknowledge and emphasize that faculty and staff occupying marginalized social locations themselves encounter a number of forms of inequity and violence in the academy (Arnold, Crawford, and Khalifa 2016; Daniel 2019; Hanasono et al. 2019; Henry et al. 2017; Joseph and Hirshfield 2011; Mayuzumi 2015; Pittman 2010)—some of which may echo the violence experienced by students while others of which may be particular to their faculty or staff roles. Similarly, pedagogical partnership may offer exciting possibilities for redressing some of the harms equity-seeking faculty and staff experience (Cook-Sather 2020), as well as additional challenges and tensions for faculty and staff that we do not explore in this book (Marquis, Guitman et al. 2020; Marquis, Woolmer et al. 2019). Again, we hope this work provides a starting point for further investigation of such issues, and we invite others to join us in considering if and how the ideas and arguments we offer might be applied, extended, and altered to better understand if and how partnership might contribute to redressing the harms experienced by faculty and staff in postsecondary institutions.

In writing this book, we seek to encourage and contribute to the development of theories of pedagogical partnership in general and in relation to equity-focused impacts, and to affirm the urgency of work that opens up alternate ways of thinking, feeling, being, relating, and moving to advance justice. As Alexis Giron emphasized in the book's foreword, when we name the problem of inequity and injustice more clearly and specifically, using stronger and more precise words like *epistemic, affective, and ontological violence*, we are aided in recognizing, condemning, and acting to redress the harms that result. We hope this work bolsters our collective commitment to naming the violences and redressing the resulting harms that marginalized groups face in postsecondary education by offering conceptual and concrete tools we can think and act with to bring about change. The application of our conceptual framework to the pedagogical partnership literature models and supports this change, even as it raises questions for further consideration and exploration. Both such support and such perpetual interrogation are essential to working for equity and justice.

# A CONCEPTUAL FRAMEWORK FOR REDRESSING HARMS AND WORKING TOWARD EQUITY AND JUSTICE THROUGH PARTNERSHIP

In this chapter, we introduce our conceptual framework of epistemic, affective, and ontological violences experienced by equity-seeking students within postsecondary education and the harms that result, drawing on students' own words about their experiences and on the work of theorists that helps us understand these lived realities. Although some of the words we draw on are from students in pedagogical partnership, most are from students quoted in research on the inequities that marginalized students experience. These students' words, then, evoke the larger context of (in)equity and (in)justice in which we situate this book and to which we argue partnership might respond. As Iverson (2007) has asserted, "How the problem is framed determines the range of solutions available; in turn, it also conceals from view an array of options that could emerge from alternate conceptions of the problem" (605). By theorizing the problem of equity-seeking students' experiences through the framework of epistemic, affective, and ontological violences and resulting harms, we believe that particular nuances and dimensions of those students' struggles become more clearly defined and perceptible.

To identify the epistemic, affective, and ontological harms caused by forms of violence within postsecondary institutions and that pedagogical partnerships begin to redress, we started by identifying patterns in the ways that participants in partnership have described its benefits and impacts, and then traced these back to identify underlying forms of violence and resulting harms that partnership is positioned to counter. Expanding on our introduction of these ideas in chapter 1, we explain in this chapter our three primary reasons for focusing on these forms of violence and harm.

First, the typical approaches to seeking equity and justice in postsecondary education institutions tend to occur at legislative and "material" levels that often miss and fail to respond to epistemic, affective, and ontological injustice (de Bie et al. 2019; Fricker 2007; Stauffer 2015; Thomas 2007). For example, institutions have often focused on abiding by human rights, accessibility, and employment equity legislation or improving material "access" to education in the first place. These strategies might ensure compliance with requirements and seek to redistribute the resources of the institution in more equitable ways, but they might not engage with other layers of (in)equity and (in)justice. Indeed, Gibson (2015), writing about inclusion for disabled students in UK postsecondary education institutions, has noted that such institutions remain highly inequitable in spite of developments in human rights legislation and policy, and has argued for the need for "post-rights" strategies for inclusive education.

Second, although we may abstractly know what some forms of violence are, "those who have never been . . . dehumanized [or faced other specific violences] may lack the kind of understanding that brings to fore the *harms* of these crimes" (Stauffer 2015, 12, emphasis in original). For this reason we specifically focus on articulating the harms endured by students from equity-seeking groups as a result of epistemic, affective, and ontological violences, as those who have not experienced these harms themselves may be less able to understand them. This insufficient understanding of harms endured may be further exacerbated in a context where forms of violence—like epistemic, affective, ontological ones—are themselves less known and recognized. Consequently, we write about both *violence* (what is done by institutions and individuals to preserve dominant structures and processes)—and we use the plural *violences* to signal that there are multiple forms—and investigate and dwell in the *harms* (the experiences) such violence provokes for equity-seeking students. Within this chapter, we sometimes refer to *injustice* as the characterization of both violence inflicted and the harms that result, as this is the language used by some theorists whose work anchors our conceptualizations.

Third, partnership approaches emphasize the importance of respectful and reciprocal interpersonal relationships (Cook-Sather, Bovill, and Felten 2014), which often have an impact at epistemic, affective, and ontological levels and are thus well suited to addressing these otherwise obscured or minimized injustices and resulting harms. Although partnership and its capacity to effect change at epistemic, affective, and ontological levels is the subject of this book, we offer partnership practice and its theorization as one strategy for (although not the single solution to) redressing the harms that result from various forms of violence inflicted by postsecondary education, and we encourage the exploration of other approaches that address these less materially tangible forms of harm.

In presenting this conceptual framework here, and extending it to consider the work of pedagogical partnership in redressing epistemic, affective, and ontological harms in chapter 3, we draw on a number of sources. These include student experiences quoted in published research that we and others have conducted, unpublished data from three ethics-board-approved studies (see Appendix A), and works in progress. These sources revealed multiple examples of violence (what is inflicted by postsecondary education on equity-seeking students) and resulting harms (what students experience) that partnership has the potential to address. Although we treat each form of violence inflicted and harm experienced "separately," our subsequent discussion demonstrates how intricately connected they are and how, we propose, partnership can contribute to redressing them.

## Epistemic Violences and Harms

Epistemic violence, which has been discussed and documented by marginalized groups for generations, manifests itself by deeming some knowledge and knowers as legitimate and, by doing so, disqualifying other knowledge and people as subknowers (Kidd, Medina, and Pohlhaus 2017; May 2014; Spivak 1988). Such violence, when perpetrated on students with marginalized identities in postsecondary education institutions, can result in epistemic harms. Figure 2.1 represents epistemic violences inflicted on and harms experienced by students in postsecondary education.

One expression of epistemic harm is that the expertise of students from equity-seeking groups and their value as knowers often go unrecognized, resulting in these students not being given the epistemic credit they deserve (Kotzee 2017). Students have commonly reported feeling undermined by

**Figure 2.1.** Epistemic violences inflicted on and harms experienced by students in postsecondary education.

| Epistemic Violences | Epistemic Harms |
|---|---|
| Equity-seeking students' <br> • knowledge and capacity as knowers are discounted <br> • diverse epistemologies (e.g., experiential, familial, nondominant cultural knowledge) are not recognized <br> • epistemic labor is dismissed and/or exploited | Equity-seeking students <br> • feel unrecognized as knowers <br> • experience their diverse epistemologies as illegitimate <br> • experience their epistemic labor as invisible and not valued, or as unfairly used |

their instructors and peers who perceive them as "stupid," incapable, and lacking academic ability: "Just like in classes or student organizing where they feel like you're simply just not qualified without hearing you out, or just kind of assum[e] that you are . . . not able to" (Muslim student quoted in Alizai 2017, 58). "I . . . feel no one wants to be in the same group with me," a Chinese student explained to her interviewer, "[b]ecause they probably think, OK, this girl, English is not her first language. She probably didn't know what she's doing. And they probably think they have to carry my weight" (student quoted in Lo 2016, 120, emphasis removed).

A significant consequence of this epistemic injustice is that students from equity-seeking groups receive fewer opportunities to contribute to knowledge production and exchange. As a Latino student explained, compared to their White peers, "It's very difficult for me to go up to a professor and ask him questions" (quoted in Yosso et al. 2009, 668). Other students may withhold their ideas in class: "I don't feel that what I say makes a difference. I don't feel what I say is relevant. I feel what I say is considered to be stupid, therefore I don't want to talk" (Chinese student quoted in Lo 2016, 163, emphasis removed). Fricker (2007) characterized these forms of epistemic harm as *testimonial,* where an identity-related prejudice (e.g., related to one's identity as a student and/or member of equity-seeking communities) leads to being wronged in one's capacity as a knower.

A second form of violence is when students' experiential, familial, and other forms of nondominant cultural knowledge are not counted as valuable and not considered worth being known (Pohlhaus 2017). This form of violence results in the harm of equity-seeking students experiencing their diverse epistemologies as illegitimate. As one student explained: "The classroom and academia . . . values objectivity, methods, facts, and conclusions over truth and stories. I must say even in classes about identity, I still am performing as a nonnormative figure, a black woman" (student quoted in Study 3, Appendix A). A Latinx student similarly described how "I came to college and I was made to believe, although I never accepted it, that what I knew, that what my brothers in my 'hood knew, did not have a place here" (student quoted by Padilla 1997 in Pizarro 1998, 66). When students gain knowledge through participation in equity-seeking groups, this may be seen as "limiting" rather than a rich source of expertise:

> I'm pretty involved with different aspects of the Latino community at school here. And [a White friend] implied that my involvement in these communities and activities were kind of reflective of me limiting myself. And [that] in a certain way, I was trying to take the easy way out, by studying Latin American history. (Student quoted in Yosso et al. 2009, 677)

Some students may be pushed as far as to abandon their ways of knowing: "I went to school with all of my treasures, including my Spanish language, Mexican culture, familia (family), and ways of knowing. I abandoned my treasures at the classroom door in exchange for English and the U.S. culture" (del Carmen Salazar 2013, 121). When the culture of the academy gives more credence to students from epistemically privileged groups, creates and teaches a curriculum based on these perspectives, or fails to understand the perspectives of equity-seeking students, these are examples of the dominant society lacking interpretive tools for recognizing and valuing diverse epistemologies (Kotzee 2017). This is a "hermeneutical" form of epistemic violence, where there is an inability to make sense of an experience (e.g., non-dominant knowledges) due to a gap in available tools for the interpretation of social meanings (Fricker 2007).

③ The last form of epistemic violence taken up by our framework occurs when marginalized students' epistemic labor is dismissed or exploited. This leads to the harm of equity-seeking students feeling invisible and as though their efforts are disregarded or used unfairly, such as when they challenge oppression in the classroom. For example, students have described feeling unheard by their classmates when speaking about equity issues. Maria, an undergraduate student who identifies as queer, genderqueer, Latina/Chicana, and with disability, was disrespected when sharing her knowledge in class: *"your credibility is taken away, and nobody wants to listen"*; instead, other students have conveyed the attitude *"Oh, there's [Maria] talking again, about her whatever"* (Miller 2015, 386, emphasis in original). Similarly, Farida's effort to address Islamophobic comments in class received the response: "Farida let people talk, let other people say something" (student quoted in Alizai 2017, 50). Furthermore, even when students from equity-seeking groups are not making an intervention into classroom dynamics, they may be perceived as doing so and have their perspective dismissed as representative of a social group to which they belong:

> I have been accused once by this guy [in a tutorial] when I was debating. . . . I give an opinion and this guy said that "you only give that opinion because you're a Muslim, and because you can't think outside of that." (Student quoted in Alizai 2017, 55)

The requirement that students challenge otherwise unaddressed injustices can be considered epistemic exploitation, or "unrecognized, uncompensated, emotionally taxing, coerced epistemic labour" (Berenstain 2016, 570; see also Mercer-Mapstone, Islam, and Reid 2021). Such exploitation might be seen in the following example, in which a student participant in a study by Gonzales et al. (2015) experienced a classroom discussion as oppressive due to the assumed link between illness and criminality, and spoke up to address it:

> [In class] we were talking about . . . if . . . people with mental illness are more likely to commit crime. And I piped up. I said, "Well, I have a mental illness. I'm bipolar. And I don't feel the need to commit a crime." (5)

Although this student ultimately found it empowering to disclose her illness to disprove a stereotype, this requirement to perform unrecognized epistemic labor to respond to a marginalizing classroom environment could constitute a form of exploitation.

Taken together, these manifestations of epistemic violence inflict a variety of harms, where students from equity-seeking groups are discounted as knowers, have their diverse epistemologies ignored and devalued, and experience their epistemic labor as dismissed, not valued, or exploited, especially when seeking to advance equity and justice.

## Affective Violences and Harms

Although violence is perhaps most readily understood as assaults on one's bodily autonomy or freedom, scholars and activists have called us to hold space and create new languages for understanding affective violence in society (Whynacht 2017). Figure 2.2 represents affective violences inflicted on and harms experienced by students in postsecondary education.

Affective violence has been theorized through several interrelated conceptions, which we review later in this subsection. The affective harms of this form of violence are well evident in student accounts that describe student discomfort, isolation, exhaustion, uncertainty, nonbelonging, feelings

**Figure 2.2.** Affective violences inflicted on and harms experienced by students in postsecondary education.

| Affective Violences | Affective Harms |
| --- | --- |
| Equity-seeking students<br>• are subject to multiple forms of discrimination and oppression (e.g., psycho-emotional disablism; microaggressions and abuse)<br>• are expected to conform to dominant norms | Equity-seeking students<br>• experience emotional effects of discrimination and oppression (e.g., isolation, nonbelonging, self-doubt, uncertainty, fatigue)<br>• carry burdens of emotional labor |

of being misunderstood, and other difficult emotions as a result of inequity and exclusion. Such affective harms are also evident in the burden of emotional labor students from equity-seeking groups carry. We start with students' descriptions of these experiences.

Students have described a range of emotional repercussions from experiences of discrimination and oppression. Illustrating the emotional effects of being trans in a potentially unwelcoming classroom space, one student quoted in Austin et al. (2019) described feeling uncomfortable identifying themselves to their peers and instructor because, based on the classroom culture around trans issues, "I think they would all misunderstand me. I really don't feel like dealing with the questions and being the 'freak' in the class" (916). Another student explained how "it can be a very isolating experience" (Austin et al. 2019, 916) to be trans and gay among their cisgender heterosexual classmates. Facing different challenges, a student described her exhaustion defending herself in the classroom: "I get tired of proving my [Indigenous] identity and having to defend it. . . . I like shut down a little bit. It's exhausting. Why do I want to keep doing it?" (student quoted in Masta 2018, 828). As a final example, a student partner reflected on her feelings of not fitting in as an international student whose first language is not English: "My identity, my beliefs, my worries, and my sense of uncertainty as I navigated the unfamiliar academic spaces of Haverford College all contributed to my sense of not belonging" (Colón García 2017, 1).

Addressing a second form of affective harm equity-seeking students experience, students have reported the significant labor involved in managing their emotional expressions, such as feeling unable to express difficult emotions for fear of being labeled as the "angry student of color" or "unhappy queer" (Abustan 2017, 40). In focus groups with Muslim students, staff, and faculty on one of our campuses, participants described "feeling pressure to act in ways that make other people feel comfortable or make themselves appear likeable." Concerned about being perceived as dangerous or a threat, they also recounted "feel[ing] the need to project a happy and friendly Muslim image" (Equity and Inclusion Office 2017, 16).

The affective harms introduced by these student accounts can be further understood with the support of a number of associated conceptual frameworks. Developed within disability studies, the concept of psycho-emotional disablism draws attention to the emotional effects of disability oppression (Reeve 2012), which others have similarly theorized as "psychological oppression" (Bartky 1990, 22). These emotional effects of oppression are profound: "The damage inflicted works along psychological and emotional pathways, impacting negatively on self-esteem, personal confidence, and ontological security. Disabled people can be made to feel worthless, useless, of lesser value, ugly, burdensome (Reeve, 2002, 2006)" (Thomas 2007, 72). Others have conceptualized the everyday insults, indignities, and acts of dehumanization—often subtle and unintentional, but not exclusively— that people from marginalized groups experience as "microaggressions," and have identified a range of related emotional effects: anger, embarrassment, invalidation, rejection, loneliness, self-doubt, unimportance, invisibility, and feeling less than human (Clark et al. 2014; Poolokasingham et al. 2014; Suárez-Orozco et al. 2015; Wing Sue 2010). As we noted in chapter 1, some scholars have insisted on stronger language to name such experiences:

> I do not use "microaggression" anymore. I detest the post-racial platform that supported its sudden popularity. I detest its component parts—"micro" and "aggression." A persistent daily low hum of racist abuse is not minor. I use the term "abuse" because aggression is not as exacting a term. Abuse accurately describes the action and its effects on people: distress, anger, worry, depression, anxiety, pain, fatigue, and suicide. (Kendi 2019, 47)

Additionally, scholars have referred to the "minority stress" (not belonging, feeling like an imposter) that students from marginalized communities experience (Cokley et al. 2013). This can come from "belonging uncertainty," defined as "doubt as to whether one will be accepted or rejected by key figures in the social environment," which can "prove acute if rejection could be based on one's negatively stereotyped social identity" (Cohen and Garcia 2008, 365). As Gopalan and Brady (2019) detailed in the first nationally representative sample of first-year students in U.S. colleges, students from underrepresented racial-ethnic minorities (e.g., Black, Hispanic, and Native) and first-generation college backgrounds have reported lower sense of belonging as well as greater uncertainty about their belonging (Strayhorn 2012; Walton and Cohen 2007). Students have also experienced "fatigue"—racial battle fatigue, burnout, and compassion fatigue (Franklin, Smith, and Hung 2014; Linder et al. 2019; Smith et al. 2016; Vaccaro and Mena 2011). In short, there are many efforts to politicize and collectivize marginalized students' affective states—and to understand them as resulting from structures of oppression as opposed to individual biology or other innate deficit.

## Ontological Violences and Harms

Epistemic and affective violences, separately and together, constitute and are constituted by ontological forms of violence. When equity-seeking students' knowledge and capacity as knowers are discounted, when their diverse epistemologies are not recognized, and when their epistemic labor is dismissed, they not only experience the harms of feeling unrecognized, illegitimate, and invisible. They can internalize these forms of harm and, for instance, experience loss of confidence in their knowledge (e.g., others believe them incapable and they come to believe this themselves), which can affect their sense of self as a knower, preventing them from knowing what they might have known or being who they might have been (Fricker 2007). Likewise, when equity-seeking students are subject to multiple forms of discrimination and oppression and expected to conform to dominant norms, they not only experience resulting emotional harms and the burdens of emotional labor. They can also internalize those harms, triggering ontological harms that impact their vision of who they are and can be. Hipolito-Delgado (2010) illustrated this internalization as follows: "The effects of racism go beyond the immediate feelings of shame, fear, or anger. Rather, the long-term effects of racism damage the inner well-being of Chicana/o and Latina/o students and promote ethnic self-hatred" (328). That is, affective harms from social injustice can have ontological repercussions. Perhaps most significantly, when equity-seeking students' very beings are negated or inhibited and when these students are blocked from being themselves, their sense of "who they are" is undermined and can have a devastating impact on their agency: "Being in a situation where one's self is not validated in good enough relationships and contexts leads to a loss of a sense of self, and of agency and desire" (Mann 2001, 12). Figure 2.3 represents ontological violences inflicted on and harms experienced by students in postsecondary education.

**Figure 2.3.** Ontological violences inflicted on and harms experienced by students in postsecondary education.

| Ontological Violences | Ontological Harms |
|---|---|
| • Epistemic and affective violences constitute and are constituted by ontological violences<br>• Equity-seeking students are dehumanized—their very beings are negated or inhibited, blocking them from being who they are<br>• Normalized and institutionalized academic ontologies restrict possibilities for being | Equity-seeking students<br>• internalize epistemic harms and dehumanization (i.e., experience negative impacts on sense of self, personhood; deny and limit who they are and can be)<br>• engage in self-suppression through adaptation to dominant ontologies, becoming unable to be fully themselves<br>• experience a profound lack of agency |

To manage the forms of harm that result from ontological violences, students from equity-seeking groups may engage in various forms of self-protection that suppress who they are and their diverse range of talents and interests. Three students from varied equity-seeking groups explained:

> I'd cultured my own behaviour in a way of . . . pretty much whatever the nondisabled students I was around felt like doing, I'd sort of modify my behaviour so that it gels with what's going on. (Student quoted in Water-meyer 2009, 271)

> I tend to keep my [disability-related] accommodations a secret. . . . As a learner I think my experience is sometimes hindered because I feel as if I am living a double life. (Student quoted in Marquis, Fudge Schormans et al. 2016, 57)

> On campus I feel like I have to put up a facade, and walk around with it so people don't "fuck with me." I use it to protect myself, because as soon as I let it down, I feel like my identity will be attacked. . . . I always find myself having to bite off/cut off my tongue to feel respected in this [college] community. (Student quoted in Cook-Sather, Des-Ogugua, and Bahti 2018, 380)

These forms of suppression may leave students unable to be fully themselves, a form of ontological harm, in order to adapt to the culture of the university (Mann 2001; Martin 2008).

Offering an example of how all of the forms of ontological harm we discuss here can intersect, Averi, an agender, queer, asexual, nonablebodied, Jewish student activist quoted by Linder et al. (2019), explained: "I was just completely destroyed as a human in almost every way [in my] two years that I spent at [institution]. . . . Everyone just repeatedly told me I wasn't worth it and what I did was stupid" (55). Personhood and our sense of self is not developed in isolation; it is cooperatively authored and impacted by the people around us. Consequently, when we are dehumanized or unsupported by those with whom we are in relationship, as Averi described, our worlds and selves can be destroyed (Stauffer 2015).

These examples illustrate the importance of Carol Thomas's (1999) provocation to investigate how oppression affects "who we *are*" (46) and how we think about ourselves in order to attend to the ontological violences and resulting harms that negatively impact our possibilities for *being*, instead of only the restrictions that oppression poses on what marginalized people can *do* (e.g., through inequitable access to education or employment). Injustice at the level of ontology is elaborated by Wilson (2017) as follows:

> Where epistemological injustice may be described as the exclusion of alternative views of the world, ontological injustice is concerned with the exclusion of views of alternative worlds (Viveiros de Castro, 2013). . . . Furthermore, it is not just that the worlds are different, but that they are differently and unequally valued. (1083)

As the last component of our conceptual framework, albeit one that is intimately interwoven with the epistemic and affective components described earlier, ontological violences as we understand them operate in a range of ways and cause a range of harms. For example, Daly (2000), taking a Marxist perspective, has argued that capitalism could be interpreted as an ontological form of violence and injustice "because it prevents people from becoming fully human by emphasizing their labour as the key aspect of their identity" (Wilson 2017, 1083, referring to Daly 2000). The dominant ontology of postsecondary education, where students are turned into numbers, seen as commodities, and expected to develop into "independent" scholars and compete against each other for individual achievement and success (Cates, Madigan, and Reitenauer 2018), has also been critiqued as dehumanizing, alienating, and neglectful (Kahn 2017; Mann 2001; Martin 2008; Willimon and Naylor 1995). It separates students from essential aspects of themselves as persons and their "vocation of becoming more fully human" (Freire 1970, 44, quoted in Reyes and Villarreal 2016, 548), and fails to recognize a broader range of student aspirations, needs, and corresponding ways of being (Kahn 2017). Although these dominant ontologies affect all students (and staff and faculty), they may be especially impactful, in negative ways, for students historically underrepresented in postsecondary education—due to dissonance between academic ontologies and those of family or community and persistent inequities in any "competitive" process that tends to privilege particular groups.

The harms that result from students internalizing these educational norms and practices are also multiple. As Mann (2001) has argued, "The demands of learning the language of rational, abstracting, academic discourse and processes may require the student to repress their being as non-rational, creative, unconscious and desiring selves, the very selves which they may need for engaging in learning" (12). These ontological demands endemic to academic culture override other ontologies and ways of being—such as those that encourage more collaborative, interdependent, and process-driven ways of producing knowledge and relating to each other. The conceptualization of internalized oppression (also theorized as internalized "isms" like internalized racism, internalized ableism, etc.) furthers this discussion, highlighting how students from equity-seeking groups can, often unconsciously, absorb

oppressive societal beliefs of their inferiority and incapability into their consciousness, impacting their sense of self, their agency (e.g., beliefs in their
own moral judgment and autonomous capacity to act in the world), and perceptions of who they can be (Bartky 1990; Hipolito-Delgado 2010; Irizarry
and Raible 2014; Liebow 2016).

## Conclusion

We hope this framework helps make the violences inflicted on students from
equity-seeking groups more clearly defined and perceptible so that we can
explore in chapter 3 the multiple ways that pedagogical partnership may
assist us in redressing the associated harms. When we fail to directly name
violences and corresponding harms in the institution, we divert responsibility for addressing them and thus contribute to their maintenance (Patton
et al. 2019).

The conceptual framework we develop and apply asks us to reconsider
equity and justice as more than "additions" or "enhancements" to a neutral
state, and discourages approaches designed to be universally applied to the
student body. Indeed, authors like Patton et al. (2019) have critiqued an
abundance of so-called "diversity" initiatives in postsecondary education that
are geared toward benefiting "all students" as opposed to shifting systems of
disadvantage. Instead, we argue that there are urgent and specific epistemic,
affective, and ontological forms of violence faced by students from equity-
seeking groups that lead to harms we are called on to redress. Legislative and
policy approaches to addressing social inequities are important, but inadequate on their own. We must also develop ways of recognizing epistemic,
affective, and ontological forms of violence on campus and redressing the
harms they cause (de Bie 2019a, 2019b).

This work has several tensions and limitations, to which we turn in
chapter 5. But first we focus, in chapter 3, on how the growing body of
scholarship on pedagogical partnership can be reseen within the conceptual
framework we have offered, and in chapter 4 we present two case studies in
the terms the framework affords. In both these chapters we aim to illustrate
how pedagogical partnership can redress epistemic, affective, and ontological
harms and actively pursue equity and justice in these interrelated spheres of
student experience.

Gonzales (2015) has argued that efforts to facilitate epistemic justice
must be foundational to equity work in postsecondary education:

> Working towards epistemic justice is, I believe, the ultimate form of affirma-
> tive action that colleges and universities can commit to as it advances equity

beyond structural or numerical counts, and instead commits to equity in terms of the core purposes of higher education: teaching, learning, and the production of knowledge. (38)

We agree, and would add that working toward affective and ontological justice is also essential to this project. The remainder of our analysis thus illuminates how pedagogical partnerships can offer a "location of possibility" (Cates, Madigan, and Reitenauer 2018) for advancing equity beyond considerations of access and inclusion, and may play an important role in bringing about epistemic, affective, and ontological justice within the core purposes of postsecondary education.

# 3

# REDRESSING EPISTEMIC, AFFECTIVE, AND ONTOLOGICAL HARMS THROUGH PARTNERSHIP

A growing body of work has suggested that partnership has the potential to contribute to countering the harms marginalized students experience as a result of epistemic, affective, and ontological violences, though this conceptual framing is not typically drawn on or made explicit in partnership research and practice. Some partnership programs are launched specifically with a focus on fostering greater equity and inclusion (e.g., Cook-Sather 2018a; Cook-Sather, Bahti, and Ntem 2019; Cook-Sather, Ortquist-Ahrens, and Reynolds 2019; Leota and Sutherland 2020), for example, and many ground their partnership projects and analyses in critical race and feminist theory (e.g., Cates, Madigan, and Reitenauer 2018; Chukwu and Jones 2020; Cook-Sather and Agu 2013; Guitman, Acai, and Mercer-Mapstone 2020; Mercer-Mapstone and Mercer 2018). Considering these examples—and indeed much of the scholarship on partnership more broadly—in relation to our conceptual framework begins to make clear that partnership might contribute to equity in postsecondary education in a broader range of ways than is typically considered. Likewise, this framework also points to additional questions, tensions, and areas of concern that partnership scholars and practitioners interested in equity and justice might consider going forward.

Thus far, the partnership literature has tended to characterize the problem of inequity in the university in three primary ways. The first cluster involves work that has focused on the enriching "benefit" of partnership to student engagement and the affirmation of student experience and knowledge, against a neutral background or one without explicit recognition of violence inflicted on and harm experienced by many students, particularly those from equity-seeking groups. In essence, such literature has implied that the basic function of the university is benign, but could be greatly enhanced through partnership. The second cluster includes scholarship that has recognized (sometimes implicitly) all students as being harmed by virtue of the student–faculty power hierarchy in, or other practices of, the academy. We might include here, for instance, partnership work that has been critical of the neoliberal emphasis on competition, commodification, and the positioning of students as customers—an emphasis that resonates with the ontological violences discussed in chapter 2, which harm all students by limiting possibilities for who they are and might become. Partnerships seek to address this universally shared form of harm across the student population by creating more egalitarian, reciprocal, humanizing relationships (Cook-Sather and Felten 2017a; Cook-Sather and Porte, 2017). Work in this category has often also attended to the difficulty of working across power differences and attempting to mitigate hierarchies attached to institutional roles, gesturing to both the potential of partnership to redress oppressive relationships and its limitations in this regard, as well as to the reality that institutionally and socially accorded power doesn't simply disappear when partnerships are initiated (Goldsmith and Gervasio 2011; Guitman, Acai, and Mercer-Mapstone 2020; Kehler, Verwoord, and Smith 2017; Mihans, Long, and Felten 2008; Seale et al. 2015; Verwoord and Smith 2020).

The third cluster is composed of research and reflective writing more immediately aligned with the framework we advance in chapter 2. It includes examples that have recognized particular harms to students from equity-seeking groups (often alongside recognition of general harms that other students may also face), and positioned partnership as offering a unique and important redress of the harms these students experience. In this cluster, injustice has often been acknowledged in broad strokes, with limited discussion of the specific harms it entails.

In this chapter, we aim to build on work in the latter two categories by explicitly naming and focusing on pursuing epistemic, affective, and ontological justice and considering how some of the outcomes and possibilities noted in the partnership literature might be read and fleshed out in relation to this particular approach to realizing equity.

## Partnership and Epistemic Justice

Partnership facilitates justice via redress of the harms resulting from forms of epistemic violence. Specifically, partnership affirms students, especially those from equity-seeking groups, as knowers; recognizes students' knowledge gained from diverse backgrounds and experiences; and develops and shares students' knowledge, which can, in turn, facilitate broader change. Figure 3.1 reproduces the epistemic violences and harms presented in

Figure 2.1 in chapter 2. In the third column, it additionally represents partnership's facilitation of justice via redress of the harms resulting from epistemic violences.

**Figure 3.1.** Partnership's facilitation of justice via redress of the harms resulting from epistemic violences.

| Epistemic Violences | Epistemic Harms | Epistemic Justice |
|---|---|---|
| Equity-seeking students' <br>• knowledge and capacity as knowers are discounted <br>• diverse epistemologies are not recognized <br>• epistemic labor is dismissed or exploited | Equity-seeking students <br>• feel unrecognized as knowers <br>• experience their diverse epistemologies as illegitimate <br>• experience their epistemic labor as invisible and not valued, or as unfairly used | Partnership enables <br>• affirmation of students, especially those from equity-seeking groups, as knowers <br>• recognition of students' knowledge gained from diverse backgrounds and experiences <br>• the development and sharing of students' knowledge, which can, in turn, facilitate broader change |

In many ways, partnership practices are predicated on recognizing and affirming students as "holders and creators of knowledge" (Delgado Bernal 2002, 106), and thus inherently (if not always explicitly) interconnected with epistemic possibilities, including redress of the harm that comes from having one's knowledge, ways of knowing, and/or epistemic labor discounted. Indeed, attention to epistemic justice implicitly underpins two of the most common definitions of *pedagogical partnership* in the literature:

> A collaborative, reciprocal process through which all participants have the opportunity to contribute equally, although not necessarily in the same ways, to curricular or pedagogical conceptualization, decision-making, implementation, investigation, or analysis. (Cook-Sather, Bovill, and Felten 2014, 6–7)

A process of student engagement, understood as staff and students learning and working together to foster engaged student learning and engaging learning and teaching enhancement. In this sense partnership is a relationship in which all participants are actively engaged in and stand to gain from the process of learning and working together. (Healey, Flint, and Harrington 2014, 7)

In these excerpts, it is clear that the goal of partnership is to invite students into knowledge production practices—where they are recognized and affirmed as knowers and encouraged and supported to contribute. Partnerships intentionally address the "testimonial" (Fricker 2007) form of epistemic injustice that students experience—where their knowledge is discounted due to their position as a student.

Likewise, a wide variety of scholarship has documented examples in which partnership works to recognize and value students' knowledge, and to engage students actively in knowledge production and exchange (e.g., Cook-Sather and Porte 2017; Dunne and Zandstra 2011; Pallant 2014; Wang and Jiang 2012)—processes that again affirm their status as knowers. Participating students have detailed the active and significant roles partnership enables them to play in knowledge generation (rather than just passive receipt of others' knowledge), for instance, underlining the potentially transformative nature of this shift:

> I could not believe that I was being given access to these documents, that I had the right to do my research in such a legitimate way. I felt like a researcher, not just a student working for a grade. Holding these pieces of history gave new weight to the work that I was doing. Though I had done so much research on the computer, I had not experienced the documents in such an emotional way. It made everything I was researching real. Sharing this moment with Rhiannon [Cates] was a powerful experience, as she was as excited as I was to share the moment with me. After our trip to Special Collections, I fully committed to my project with the belief that I was a researcher with the power to learn something and to say something. This was real agency. (Mariah Madigan [student partner] in Cates, Madigan, and Reitenauer 2018, 41)

Likewise, many students have described feeling like their perspectives, experiences, and knowledges are valued within their partnerships, sometimes contrasting this to previous experiences in the academy in which this was decidedly not the case:

> For this project, it was very different . . . you feel like you're more on the same level as the rest of the team and you feel actually heard, and you feel like people actually care about your perspective and about your unique background. (Student quoted in Cook-Sather et al. 2019, 25)

> [As a result of the destabilization of power dynamics in partnership work] I feel so much more ownership over my experience as a student. I feel like I've been given a platform to say, "No, I know things and I need things and other people also need things, and I can be in tune with that." (Student quoted in de Bie et al. 2019, 40)

Some of this work (including the pieces from which the last two quotations are drawn) has focused specifically on the importance of these processes for students from underrepresented and marginalized groups, who have often experienced the kinds of harms from epistemic violences described in chapter 2 (Burns, Sinfield, and Abegglen 2019; Cook-Sather and Agu 2013; Cook-Sather and Luz 2015; Cook-Sather et al. 2019; de Bie et al. 2019; O'Shea 2018; Mercer-Mapstone, Guitman, and Acai 2019; Moys 2018).

Although this kind of epistemic recognition through partnership can be a powerful thing, given the entrenchment of epistemic marginalization and violence so many students experience, it is not always straightforward or guaranteed. Several student partners have recounted initial or ongoing experiences of uncertainty and doubt within their partnerships, for example, and in some cases have explained that they need to "unlearn" internalized conceptions that their knowledge isn't valuable (de Bie et al. 2019). (We discuss this tension in detail in chapter 5.) Considering such experiences within the frame of epistemic injustice specifically, we have argued elsewhere (de Bie et al. 2019) that partnership can be a means of helping to foster the growth of epistemic confidence for students from equity-seeking groups. Although it may not completely or easily overturn the harmful effects of long-term epistemic violence, then, partnership can be a way of encouraging both students and faculty to begin to recognize students—and particularly those who identify as members of equity-seeking groups—as legitimate knowers. Reflecting this possibility, one student partner noted:

> I am more confident in what I know: I know what I experience and there is value in that. . . . And that's been really helpful in my relationships with other professors. I get to bring up the conversation. I get to be a part of it. I don't have to have all the answers, but I do know more than I thought I did. (Student quoted in de Bie et al. 2019, 42)

In addition to contributing to the redress of epistemic harms equity-seeking students experience, this kind of epistemic recognition also has the potential to contribute to broader changes that affect the classroom and campus experiences of students beyond those engaged directly in partnerships themselves. Although some scholarship has rightly noted that the individual relationships involved in partnership are insufficient to produce structural and institutional change on their own (Guitman and Marquis 2020; Marquis, Woolmer et al. 2019), it is nevertheless true that empirical research and reflective writing have begun to document ways in which participating in partnership might facilitate change in both faculty and student teaching and learning practices, which has the potential to affect others (Brunson 2018; Conner 2012; Fraser et al. 2020; Marquis, Power, and Yin 2019; Mercer-Mapstone 2019; Stanway et al. 2019).

Students participating in partnership, for instance, have described carrying the confidence they develop in their own knowledge through to other educational contexts, and becoming more effective advocates and facilitators of equitable teaching and learning in the process (Cook-Sather 2018b; de Bie et al. 2019). Moreover, students and faculty who have been involved in classroom-focused partnerships have often described the ways in which students' knowledge and experiences, recognized and affirmed in their partnerships, support the development of more equitable teaching practices among faculty (Cook-Sather and Des-Ogugua 2019; Cook-Sather et al. 2019; Corbin and Diallo 2019; Le and Gorstein 2019; Lillehaugen and Cooney 2019; Marquis et al. forthcoming; Mathrani 2018; Narayanan and Abbot 2020; Perez 2016). These shifts are often facilitated by students mobilizing their own perspectives and experiences as members of marginalized groups in higher education contexts, as well as their expertise from equity-related intellectual and community work to promote reflection in their faculty partners. One student noted, for instance, that she could draw on her experiences and "influence or at least bring perspective" to faculty about issues of relevance to inclusive teaching and subsequently see "a change in the syllabus" (student quoted in Marquis et al. forthcoming).

As evidenced in the existing literature, partnership's redress of harms from epistemic violence thus has the capacity to reverberate beyond the individuals most immediately involved, as students' knowledge, and their growing confidence in that knowledge, support the development of more equitable educational practices.

## Partnership and Affective Justice

Partnership can also facilitate justice via redress of the harms resulting from affective violence. As noted in the third column of Figure 3.2, partnership can redress some of the emotional effects of oppression, offering an increased sense of belonging, confidence, empowerment, joy, and energy, among other states; create counterspaces that mitigate affective harms; provide relief from some forms of emotional labor in the academy; and enable new forms of affective relations between students and faculty (e.g., empathy, "politicized compassion" [Gibson and Cook-Sather 2020]). Figure 3.2 reproduces the affective violences and harms presented in Figure 2.2 in chapter 2. It additionally represents, in the third column, partnership's facilitation of justice via redress of the harms resulting from affective violences.

**Figure 3.2.** Partnership's facilitation of justice via redress of the harms resulting from affective violences.

| Affective Violences | Affective Harms | Affective Justice |
|---|---|---|
| Equity-seeking students <br>• are subject to multiple forms of discrimination and oppression (e.g., psycho-emotional disablism; microaggressions and abuse) <br>• are expected to conform to dominant norms | Equity-seeking students <br>• experience emotional effects of discrimination and oppression <br>• carry burdens of emotional labor | Partnership enables <br>• redress of some of the emotional effects of oppression (e.g., increased sense of confidence, empowerment, belonging, joy, and energy; creation of counterspaces that mitigate affective harms) <br>• relief from some forms of emotional labor in the academy <br>• new forms of affective relations between students and faculty (e.g., empathy, "politicized compassion" [Gibson and Cook-Sather 2020]) |

As noted previously, partnership can contribute to the growth of students' epistemic confidence; this growth likewise begins to make clear partnership's potential to redress the harms that result from affective violence as described in our conceptual model. In addition to documenting how working in partnership can enhance student confidence (epistemic or otherwise) (e.g., Cook-Sather 2018b; Cook-Sather and Luz 2015; de Bie et al. 2019; Eze 2019; Luker and Morris 2016; Mathrani 2018; Nave et al. 2018), the literature has demonstrated that partnership can frequently lead to other positive affective outcomes as well, such as bolstering students' sense of agency and empowerment or their feelings of belonging within academic spaces. Although partnership scholarship has not always used the language of violence or theorized in depth the emotional harms that students experience as a result of affective forms of violence, then, it has described how partnership can mediate some of these negative emotional effects.

Like enhanced confidence, student feelings of agency and empowerment have been commonly noted outcomes in the partnership literature (Cates,

Madigan, and Reitenauer 2018; Cook-Sather 2018b; Cook-Sather and Mejia 2018; Mercer-Mapstone, Dvorakova, Matthews et al. 2017). By virtue of being recognized in their capacity as knowers and given space to contribute meaningfully to the development of knowledge, students have often reported feeling what Madigan, speaking of her experience in a course demonstrating partnership principles, described as "real agency" (Cates, Madigan, and Reitenauer 2018, 41). Similarly, discussing their experience attending and copresenting at a teaching and learning conference, another student partner noted how "it felt pretty empowering" and "has given me a lot more confidence in being able to talk with professors and network with people" (quoted in Study 2, Appendix A). As this student (like many others) has suggested, feelings of empowerment arising from partnership activities are frequently interconnected with enhanced confidence. Participating in knowledge cocreation and exchange, and being valued for one's contributions, can counter a (systemically influenced) lack of confidence in one's own capacities and lead to a greater sense of agency and ownership that carries over into other aspects of students' education.

Additionally, a growing body of equity-focused partnership work has taken as a starting point that students from "at-risk and nondominant groups" often feel "a profound sense of both social and academic nonbelonging when they arrive on campus" (Barnett and Felten 2016, 9–10), and has demonstrated how the process of participating in collaborative, respectful relationships in which their perspectives are valued can begin to redress such feelings of "mis-fit" (Colón García 2017; Cook-Sather, Des-Ogugua, and Bahti 2018; Cook-Sather and Felten 2017b; Moore-Cherry et al. 2016). Reflective writing by student partners who identify as members of equity-seeking groups has illustrated this potential. Students have described partnership experiences that made them feel "like an integral part of the school and its processes" (Perez-Putnam 2016, 1), for instance, or "listened to and valued" and as though they mattered and "could belong in this new place" (Colón García 2017, 2–3). As another student put it,

> Participating in the partnerships program makes me feel as though my perspective on education and learning matters. All too often, when the Black girl speaks or tries to offer an intellectual analysis of issues at hand, her perspective is denied or deemed unworthy. It has been a pleasure to grow, develop, and contribute my learning perspective for the betterment of the class, the professor, and myself. Through this partnership, I have learned how to feel a sense of belonging in my other classrooms. In all honesty, I have had white, male professors that I felt did not appreciate my perspective in the learning environment. Thankfully, I have learned how to communicate in a way that tackles this issue. I believe that my participation in

the partnerships program has given me the tools to communicate in this way. I feel able to develop a sense of belonging in any institution that may deny the Black girl's perspective whether the action is backed by unconscious motives or full-on intent. (Quoted in Study 3, Appendix A)

Such feelings of belonging are beneficial in multiple ways (Gopalan and Brady 2019; Walton and Brady 2017). Research has suggested that a sense of belonging can lead students to engage more deeply with their studies and inspire them to seek out and use campus resources to a greater extent, contributing to persistence and success (Strayhorn 2012; Yeager et al. 2016), and may buffer students from stress, improving mental health (Baumeister and Leary 1995). The belonging that partnership can help foster may thus contribute to equity in several ways, redressing feelings of alterity and mis-fit as well as additional affective harms (stress, burnout), and supporting forms of engagement that lead to academic success.

Importantly, the sense of social and academic belonging reported by student partners in the preceding quotations is framed in relation to partnership experiences in which participants are recognized for their unique perspectives, knowledge, and identities, and have the opportunity to feel like they are contributing to institutional change (i.e., to epistemic and ontological forms of justice). As such, they speak to partnership's capacity to foster forms of belonging that do not require abandoning or sacrificing one's self to meet unchanging, oppressive institutional norms—that is, forms of belonging rooted in equity principles that recognize the value of difference and challenge injustice rather than belonging or inclusion through assimilation into the status quo. Nevertheless, it remains true that arguably less just forms of belonging might also be engendered through partnership, as in the case of another partnership Colón García (2017) described, in which she adapted to a faculty partner's communication style and, as a result, did not feel welcome as her whole self. Although Colón García argued that this experience still led to greater feelings of belonging for her, it suggests a potential tension to which scholars of partnership interested in equity might attend. We discuss this tension in detail in chapter 5.

For racialized students in particular, partnerships can also offer essential "counter-spaces" (Cook-Sather and Agu 2013, 273)—academic and social spaces "where deficit notions of people of color can be challenged and where a positive collegiate racial climate can be established and maintained" (Solórzano, Ceja, and Yosso 2000, 70). Such counterspaces are necessary to counterbalance "the daily barrage of racial microaggressions that [students] endure both in and outside of their classes" (Solórzano, Ceja, and Yosso 2000, 70), and thus create important opportunities for emotional relief—spaces that one Black student partner characterized as ones in which they could "breathe—sometimes for the first time that week" (Khadijah Seah, personal communication, April 1, 2020; see also Ortquist-Ahrens et al. 2021). At the same time, student partners from equity-seeking groups have also described their partnership experiences as "rewarding" (Perez-Putnam 2016, 1) and "fun" (Study 2, Appendix A)—a far cry from the kind of emotional harm often inflicted on marginalized students. As Hermsen et al. (2017) have argued, discussing the emotional nature of pedagogical partnerships more generally, "learning and studying are so much more interesting and joyful when [partnership] occurs" (1).

Alongside these opportunities for emotional relief and animation, some recent scholarship has also suggested that partnership spaces might provide opportunities to hear and recognize, and potentially ease to some extent, the burdens of emotional labor that equity-seeking students habitually experience in postsecondary contexts. Considering their experiences of partnership in relation to gender, for instance, Mercer-Mapstone, Guitman, and Acai (2019) offered the following poetic transcription:

> it would be a relief
> to be in a relational space
> where we are not perpetually excluded
> where we are not made to fight harder than our male peers for recognition
> where we can be leaders
> where we feel safe.
> I believe all these things exist because
> This is how I feel in my many nourishing partnerships
> I feel lucky
> I feel strong
> I feel *liberated*
> from my emotional labour. (4)

Such comments make clear both the emotional strain and oppression of many relationships and experiences in academia, and the sense of emotional relief or redress that partnership might provide. By creating spaces in which students are recognized, valued, and respected, partnerships can lead to feelings of nourishment, strength, and what Mercer-Mapstone described elsewhere as "a balm for . . . frustration" with postsecondary institutions (2020, 5).

Nevertheless, the emotions that partnership can evoke and the emotional demands of partnership itself are not always or only straightforwardly positive. Many people have written about the difficulties involved

with navigating power differentials or encountering resistance in partnerships, for example, though this has not always been treated explicitly as an
affective phenomenon (Bovill et al. 2016; Felten 2017; Marquis, Black,
and Healey 2017; Marquis, Puri et al. 2016; Seale et al. 2015). Although
power dynamics have often been raised in relation to faculty–student hierarchies, equity-focused partnership work has suggested that they can also
play out in relation to issues of identity and social location. When student
partners who identify as members of equity-seeking groups partner with
faculty occupying more privileged social locations, for instance, the perceived power imbalances can lead to unique, and often taxing, emotional
experiences (Marquis et al. forthcoming), particularly if students perceive
resistance from their faculty partners (Ntem and Cook-Sather 2018). As
such, while we do not want to discount the many ways in which partnership can be joyful and contribute to needed remedies for emotional harm,
we also acknowledge that difficult emotional experiences may well arise in
partnership (Cook-Sather et al. 2019) and argue that attending to these
proactively, and *hearing* and responding to them when they do occur, are
essential parts of doing partnership justly. This is another point we return
to and explore in depth in chapter 5.

Partnership may also contribute to redressing affective injustices by supporting the formation of new kinds of affective relations between students
and faculty. A common outcome of partnership described in the literature
is the development of empathy among participating faculty and students
(Filion-Murphy et al. 2015; Jensen and Bagnall 2015; Mercer-Mapstone,
Dvorakova, Matthews et al. 2017; Pounder, Hung-lam, and Groves 2016);
each comes to learn and understand more of the other's perspective, thereby
laying the groundwork for greater feelings of connection and solidarity (Cook-
Sather and Mejia 2018; Singh 2018). As Cook-Sather and Porte (2017) have
pointed out, the reciprocity involved in partnership also has the potential
to decenter affective relations that position faculty as the feeling subject and
marginalized or "hard to reach" (para. 1) students as objects of pity. Instead,
they have written, "partnership complicates the seemingly one-way reaching
out from those in a privileged center to students who are at some perceived
remove" (para. 3) and promotes a "reciprocal reaching across" (para. 1) the
spaces of partnership "to support pedagogies that turn our differences from
divides into possibilities for more life-affirming human connection" (para. 3).

This sense of connection as both life affirming and reciprocal begins to
politicize the notion of empathy so frequently mentioned in the partnership
literature, underscoring the need to acknowledge *both* faculty and students
as feeling subjects, and countering problematic conceptions of "feeling *for
others*" that reify and reproduce existing power relations. Building on this

contention, Gibson and Cook-Sather (2020) have argued that partnership can advance and support what they call "politicized compassion," generating affective relations that move beyond pity and feeling concern for others, toward a form of empathetic connection that enables solidarity and motivates action to support change. Partnerships do this by establishing a connection between people and enabling interpersonal exploration of the challenges, inequities, and harms student and faculty partners face, as well as the capacities, insights, and aspirations they bring to partnership, rather than allowing those to be distant and abstract. When faculty and students engage with one another, as people, and their lived experiences and knowledge are grounded, what might otherwise remain sympathy or pity becomes an imperative and a catalyst for action.

Such politicized compassion is thus at once a remediation of problematic expressions of emotion that remarginalize and belittle equity-seeking students, and a potential initiator of further efforts to redress injustice. Although the establishment of empathy and solidarity between faculty and students may *also* have complicated effects that mitigate efforts for social change in some respects (e.g., dampening critique or resistance by equity-seeking students [de Bie 2020; de Bie and Raaper 2019]), this potential to support more justice-oriented affective relations among students and faculty, and to provide structure and support for redressing affective harms, remains a compelling potential contribution to equity in postsecondary contexts.

## Partnership and Ontological Justice

Partnership facilitates justice via redress of the harms resulting from ontological violences in a number of ways. It rehumanizes through respecting the dignity and worth of students, especially those from equity-seeking groups. In addition, it facilitates social relationships through which students can develop—and have affirmed—their sense of self and agency and explore possibilities for who they can be. Finally, it develops and enacts different worldviews that counter dominant academic and neoliberal ontologies. Figure 3.3 reproduces the ontological violences and harms presented in Figure 2.3 in chapter 2 and represents partnership's facilitation of justice via redress of the harms resulting from ontological violences.

Insofar as it recognizes students as persons and seeks to rehumanize a dehumanizing education system (Cook-Sather 2006), partnership clearly has ontological implications. The concept of partnership as involving "reciprocal reaching across" (Cook-Sather and Porte 2017, para. 1), for instance, is predicated on an understanding that partnership can establish relationships

**Figure 3.3.** Partnership's facilitation of justice via redress of the harms resulting from ontological violences.

| Ontological Violences | Ontological Harms | Ontological Justice |
|---|---|---|
| • Epistemic and affective violences constitute and are constituted by ontological violences<br>• Equity-seeking students are dehumanized—their very beings are negated or inhibited, blocking them from being who they are<br>• Normalized and institutionalized academic ontologies restrict possibilities for being | Equity-seeking students<br>• internalize epistemic harms and dehumanization (i.e., experience negative impacts on sense of self, personhood; deny and limit who they are and can be)<br>• engage in self-suppression through adaptation to dominant ontologies, leaving students unable to be fully themselves<br>• experience a profound lack of agency | Partnership enables<br>• rehumanization through respecting the dignity and worth of students, especially those from equity-seeking groups<br>• social conditions and relationships through which students can develop—and have affirmed—their sense of self and agency and explore possibilities for who they can be<br>• development and enactment of different worldviews that counter dominant academic and neoliberal ontologies |

that affirm the humanity of everyone involved, in contrast to traditional practices that center the privileged as full human beings who know and feel and dehumanize others in the process. The common value of "respect" seen to underlie pedagogical partnerships (Cook-Sather, Bovill, and Felten 2014, 1) is one important mechanism by which partnerships contribute to redressing forms of ontological harm and realizing this "rehumanization." "Respecting [student] voices" and selves is especially important, one student partner asserted, "when your identity isn't affirmed" in the wider college context (student quoted in Cook-Sather 2020, 886). When pedagogical partnerships seek to practice the value of respect, they affirm the innate dignity and worth of students as persons. This respect is not based on the status of the student or what they can produce, but is owed to them as a human being. When students feel valued, worthy, recognized, and respected as a result of their participation in a partnership, this can have a significant impact on their sense of who they are and who they can be—characteristics of ontological justice and repair.

Likewise, when students describe gaining confidence or experiencing feelings of agency or empowerment through participating in partnership, we might understand this as having access to the social conditions and relationships they need to affirm and develop their sense of who they are. A sense of empowerment is thus both affective—one *feels* able to act and shape outcomes (Cook-Sather and Seay 2020)—and ontological—one develops a (potentially new) sense of self as powerful and agentic that was previously discouraged or disallowed. A sense of empowerment is also bolstered by epistemic forms of justice, such as when one's thoughts and knowledge are valued and affirmed. The following reflections demonstrate the ways in which recognition, respect, and the kinds of empowerment they might foster can lead to these kinds of ontological possibilities:

> Our partnership gave me power in a place I had previously felt powerless. I was able to find a stronger sense of self and to succeed when I became less isolated and began connecting with others through my research, when I was shown that my thoughts carried weight, when I was listened to and given deep respect. (Cates, Madigan, and Reitenauer 2018, 42)

> As an African American student, I used to let people tell me how I should think and act. I used to let them reprimand me for not being black in the way they'd like. Looking back on those times, I am embarrassed and vow to never let someone have that kind of power over me ever again. I attribute much of this sense of empowerment to my participation in the [SaLT program]. It made me feel like who I am is more than enough—that my identity, my thoughts, my ideas are significant and valuable. (Student quoted in Cook-Sather and Agu 2013, 276–277)

Whereas a lack of validation through supportive conditions and relationships can lead to a loss of sense of self and agency (Mann 2001), these comments suggest that pedagogical partnerships have the potential to facilitate environments where students' sense of self, capacity, and power is affirmed.

The confidence students often attribute to participating in partnership can also support them in asserting and affirming existing identities that have been marginalized in postsecondary contexts, thereby contributing to redressing the harm that results from having one's very being blocked or negated. One student partner reflected this possibility, for instance, noting that they have become "more open to coming out [as queer] to . . . more professional type of people" as a result of the confidence they developed by working in a partnership program (quoted in Study 2, Appendix A). Again, partnership's capacity to offer intertwined possibilities for affective and ontological redress becomes clear.

Belonging, in its own way, might also be seen to have ontological components and potential resonance with ontological repair. Although it is in one sense an affective outcome of participating in partnership for many people (addressing perceptions of "fit," attending to potential feelings of loneliness), it might also be seen as countering alienation and as reflecting and realizing previously unavailable understandings of self. Indeed, at a basic level, feelings of belonging reflect a new sense of *being* a member of institutional, disciplinary, or academic communities (Cook-Sather and Seay 2020). This interconnection between belonging and ontology can be seen when students participating in partnership describe developing new conceptions of themselves as scholars and educators, for example, thereby implicitly asserting feelings of connection to and inclusion in those groups. One equity-seeking student partner, for instance, noted, "I feel more like I'm an equal partner in the whole structure then, than oh, she's just like the lowly grad student. . . . I guess I'm thinking of myself less as a student and more of just as a researcher" (student quoted in de Bie et al. 2019, 43).

Considering belonging in relation to ontology also adds further urgency to the question of whether the concept of belonging reifies existing norms and practices, or, to paraphrase Colón García (2017), welcomes people for their whole selves (3). Viewed in relation to this question, the feeling of belonging not only creates possibilities for new conceptions of self, but also has the potential to affirm and recognize (or to fail to affirm and recognize) people's existing identity practices. To the extent that the belonging fostered by partnership involves this affirming of "whole selves," it again has the potential to ameliorate the harms experienced by equity-seeking students, who are often encouraged and expected to suppress their ways of being in order to adapt to the existing culture of postsecondary institutions. Of course, this does not always happen. A student partner who described feeling like they sometimes "lose a part of [themselves]" so others are able to share *their* full selves (Marquis et al. forthcoming) and a student who had to "let go" of suggestions she was making to her faculty partner regarding equitable practices in order to engage in self-protection (Ntem and Cook-Sather, 2018, 90) make clear that partnership does not *necessarily* realize the goal of affirming and responding to students' humanity. When this does happen though (as has been frequently documented in the literature), the potential to redress ontological harms is pronounced.

Partnership approaches likewise have the potential to help foster new ways of thinking about being in the academy and beyond, and thus to counter the ontological harms resulting from the neoliberal, rationalist educational norms and practices discussed in chapter 2. In contrast to dominant ontologies in postsecondary education where respect for personhood is based on individual productivity, labor, or contribution, partnership fosters a broader range of possibilities. For example, partnerships might be seen to imagine and create alternative ontologies that center on mutuality, respect, and recognition, and thus to resist the "many forces pushing for neoliberal, transactional models of education (and of life)" (Guitman and Marquis 2020, 140). In this respect, Guitman and Marquis (2020) have argued that partnership might be read as "a kind of prefigurative politics—a hugely important liminal space in which people might try out and enact new ways of thinking and being" (144). Making a similar point, Cook-Sather and Felten (2017a) have argued that partnerships constitute "'as-if' spaces—spaces within which we behave the way we want to live in the wider world of the academy" (180). Within the liminal spaces of partnership, they have suggested, we can develop and begin to realize different worldviews that stand in opposition to those typically encouraged by the institution, including those that focus on "training human capital," rather than cultivating "expanded moral sympathies, deepened democratic dispositions, and a serious sense of responsibility for the world" (Hansen 2014, 4, quoted in Cook-Sather and Felten 2017a, 180–181). Referencing hooks (1994, 207), Cates, Madigan, and Reitenauer (2018) likewise have envisioned learning as "a place where paradise can be created" (33), and have suggested that partnership has an important role to play in cultivating alternative "locations of possibility" (33).

## Conclusion

A central aim of presenting our framework and using it, in this chapter, to revisit partnership scholarship is to offer a new way of naming and looking at phenomena that have already been discussed—in some cases extensively—in partnership literature. By doing so, we hope to open up new considerations for partnership that we might otherwise overlook. First, this discussion prompts us to reflect on what we mean when we talk about "equity-focused" partnership work, or partnership work intended to enhance equity and inclusion. "Access" to partnership opportunities on its own is clearly insufficient, as is gesturing at "equity" in broad and general ways. In this writing, we more specifically think about equity in the form of redressing epistemic, affective, and ontological harms.

Second, while partnership literature often reports the benefits of involvement for students at the individual level (Matthews, Mercer-Mapstone et al. 2019; Mercer-Mapstone, Dvorakova, Matthews et al. 2017), this framework compels us to further politicize these impacts and theorize lived human experiences as recounted by students themselves. Doing so encourages us to not take commonly reported outcomes of partnership like confidence, empowerment, agency, and belonging for granted as individualized, "psychological" indicators and to instead affirm the significance of these epistemic, affective, and ontological states. In keeping with partnership philosophy, participation is not about "remediating" or "rehabilitating" students from individual distress or deficit, but rather about radically transforming our relationships with each other in ways that counter the violences of the academy and the harms that result, particularly for equity-seeking students.

Both by enacting new, countercultural kinds of relationships and practices and by affirming marginalized epistemologies, affects, and ontologies as essential and generative, then, partnership can help imagine and enact more just ways of being in the academy. In chapter 4, we offer our two programs as case studies that present one potential set of examples of what this can look like in practice. In the same way we have reread the partnership literature within our new conceptual frame, we reread our own practices in the partnership programs we have developed at Bryn Mawr and Haverford Colleges and at McMaster University. As we note throughout this chapter, we also return in chapter 5 to some of the tensions and complexities we have raised in our discussion of partnership thus far. Although these challenges are taken up separately in order to give them the space and weight they require, they certainly also apply to the case studies explored in chapter 4.

# 4

# CASE STUDIES OF TWO PROGRAMS THAT SEEK TO REDRESS HARMS AND PROMOTE EQUITY AND JUSTICE

In chapter 1 we introduced our argument, ourselves, and our approach, and we provided some context for our work, and in chapter 2 we laid out our conceptual framework that both names the forms of violence students from equity-seeking groups have experienced and the harms resulting from those experiences. In chapter 3 we applied this conceptual framework to partnership literature, resituating existing scholarship on partnership within the new terms and imperatives our framework presents. In this chapter, we aim to ground and substantiate the conceptual framework by offering case studies of our programs that illustrate how the terms of the framework can be traced and enacted in partnership practices. These programs were either designed initially with or evolved into embracing an intentional focus on contributing to equity in various areas of practice, including curricular design and redesign, pedagogical analysis and revision, the scholarship of teaching and learning (SoTL), and educational development. For each case, we provide details of the program and then link those particulars back to the terms of our conceptual framework.

## Case Study: Students as Learners and Teachers (SaLT) at Bryn Mawr and Haverford Colleges

The SaLT program was conceptualized in 2006 at Bryn Mawr and Haverford Colleges, two selective liberal arts colleges in the mid-Atlantic region of the United States. Both of these colleges have Quaker roots; enroll approximately ergraduate students from diverse socioeconomic, cultural, and al backgrounds; offer a rigorous curriculum; have high teaching arch expectations for faculty; and strive to foster a sense of independ- en id social responsibility in their students. At the time of SaLT's founding, there was no formal mechanism provided by the colleges for faculty to reflect on their teaching.

To develop the SaLT program, Alison met with groups of students who identified as belonging or allies to groups underrepresented in and underserved by higher education (Cook-Sather 2018a; Cook-Sather et al. 2019). Her goal was to gather from these students their priorities and recommendations for how to build a pedagogical partnership program that supported undergraduate students and faculty working together to create more inclusive and responsive classrooms. The pilot phase of the program, supported by a start-up grant from The Andrew W. Mellon Foundation, had this explicit focus, and the recommendation the students in the focus groups made was that the first cohort of student consultants be people of color. In the spring 2007 semester, five faculty members across the disciplines of chemistry, education, English, and psychology worked with five undergraduates, all students of color, in semester-long partnerships. Through these partnerships students observed their faculty partners' classrooms each week and met weekly for one-on-one discussions with their faculty partners to explore what faculty were already doing to make their classrooms culturally responsive and what more they could do. They also met weekly as a group with Alison in her role as director of the program to explore larger questions of culture and inclusive practice.

At the time, Alison situated this work in response to calls for culturally responsive teaching (Gay 2002; Ladson-Billings 1995) and inclusive pedagogy (Howell and Tuitt 2003; Tuitt 2003), and, drawing on the weekly conversations she had with student partners and on what the student and faculty partners shared about their work together, she generated a set of recommendations for more culturally responsive practices. Ten years later, revisiting those recommendations in an analysis called "Lessons We Still Need to Learn on Creating More Inclusive and Responsive Classrooms: Recommendations from One Student–Faculty Partnership Programme" (Cook-Sather and Des-Ogugua 2019), Alison and her student partner coauthor used theories of whiteness (Ahmed 2012; Fine 2015; McIntosh 1990) and racism (Bonilla-Silva 2018; Coates 2015; Harper and Davis 2016; Sullivan 2014), as well as more recent discussions of culturally sustaining pedagogy (Paris 2012) and inclusion (Chávez and Longerbeam 2016; Tatum 2015), to frame a re-presentation of the same recommendations for practice. Although neither at its advent nor 10 years later did Alison use the language of redressing the

FOR NEXT YEAR'S INITIATIVE

harms of epistemic, affective, and ontological violence and injustice to name the program's goals, the premise, structure, and practices of the program were—and remain—very much in keeping with those commitments.

Students of all identities and experiences choose to take on the role of student partner to faculty through the SaLT program, and in a typical year between 50% and 75% identify as belonging to one or more underrepresented groups. All student partners are paid at the top of the student payscale for every hour they spend on this work, typically 5 to 7 hours per week. Since its inception, more than 195 students and 290 faculty have participated in more than 400 partnerships, typically between 10 and 15 per semester and, more recently, during the summer. Many of these are situated in the context of a pedagogy seminar offered to all incoming faculty in their 1st year in exchange for a reduced teaching load (Cook-Sather 2016), but faculty at any point in their careers or in any role (tenure track, continuing nontenure track, visiting, postdoc) can request to work with a student partner through SaLT. When a faculty member requests a student partner, they are typically paired based almost entirely on compatibility of schedules, unless a faculty member needs a student or students with particular content knowledge (e.g., for course redesign).

There are two strands of the SaLT program—pedagogical development and revision and curriculum design and redesign—although other forms of partnership emerge in response to student and faculty interest and need (as we discuss further on in this case study). Pedagogical development and revision in the SaLT program focus on classroom practice. Most classroom-focused pedagogical partnerships take the form of semester-long (or sometimes yearlong), one-on-one collaborations through which student partners observe faculty partners' classrooms once a week, take detailed observation notes, and meet with their faculty partners weekly to discuss those notes and whatever else is happening in the faculty members' classrooms (see, e.g., Schlosser and Sweeney 2015). Although the overarching goal of the SaLT program is pursuing greater equity, individual partnerships may be more or less explicitly focused on equity, depending on the student partner's sense of faculty receptivity. For example, while classroom-focused SaLT partnerships have as a priority making classrooms more inclusive, some student partners find that this goal is better pursued without making the equity focus explicit—by striving toward equity under the umbrella of engaging and effective teaching. Some focus on specific challenges, such as making STEM classes more welcoming to underrepresented students (Mathrani 2018; Narayanan and Abbot 2020; Perez 2016), and all create spaces and structures within which students can, as one student partner explained, "use my experience as a student with certain needs and learning styles to advocate for others who might be in similar positions" (Colón García 2017, p. 2) and "[advocate] for more exercises like the ones that empowered me to feel confident in my sense of place in the classroom" (p. 3).

Curriculum design and redesign projects in the SaLT program take multiple forms: coplanning a course before it is taught; cocreating or revising while a course is unfolding; redesigning a course after it is taught; and making explicit and challenging the hidden curriculum (Brunson 2018; Cook-Sather, Bahti, and Ntem 2019). We describe two examples of curriculum-focused projects: an education course designed and taught entirely through a collaboration between a student from an underrepresented group and a faculty member, and an organic chemistry course redesigned by a team of students and a faculty member.

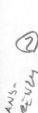

Drawing on her experience as a student consultant through SaLT, Crystal Des-Ogugua, then an undergraduate student at Bryn Mawr College, worked with Alison to codesign and coteach "Advocating Diversity in Higher Education" (Cook-Sather, Des-Ogugua, and Bahti 2018). Crystal and Alison met weekly during the semester prior to the launch of the course and codesigned every aspect of it—readings, assignments, activities. Then when the course was taught, they collaborated in its weekly planning and facilitation. A key assignment of the course was one through which Crystal (in the planning phase) and then students enrolled (while the course was unfolding) interviewed students about their identities and their experiences of inclusion and exclusion, with "anonymous portraits" of these students' experiences created by Crystal and the students enrolled in the course becoming part of the course content. The goal of the assignment was to "create a forum for marginal voices to be heard and respected by putting them in a place where they can inform classroom pedagogy and student learning" (Cook-Sather, Des-Ogugua, and Bahti 2018, 375). The particular inequity this course sought to address was the exclusion and devaluing of the lived experiences of students with dimensions of identity (e.g., racialized, first-generation, disabled, and Mad-identified students) not recognized, affirmed, or drawn upon by the traditional structures of educational institutions and classrooms. The goal of the design and teaching of the course was to create a space and structures within which students could reflect on, study, and learn from—and legitimate—both lived experiences and scholarly analyses of different dimensions of diversity.

The second example—the faculty member who taught organic chemistry at Haverford College—endeavored to address a broader, more general equity focus: the inequitable outcomes that are the result of lack of clarity and congruence among course assignments and activities in high-stakes STEM courses. The faculty member and the team of four undergraduate students who had taken the course identified seven different themes (e.g., general organization, problem sets, lectures, exams), decided to dedicate 2 weeks to exploring each theme, and scheduled weekly meetings to discuss the needs they identified within each theme and actions to meet those needs (Charkoudian et al. 2015). A specific revision the team made had to do with making more transparent the flow of the course because lack of such transparency is one source of inequity, disadvantaging a wide variety of students. Charkoudian and her team "clearly articulated key concepts/topics from each lecture and created a list of objectives ('by the end of the class you will be able to . . .') to be shared with the students at the beginning and end of each class" (Charkoudian et al. 2015, 5). The goal of this aspect—and all aspects—of the redesign was to make the assignments and activities of the organic chemistry course aligned with the purposes of the course and make "organic chemistry accessible, rather than dauntingly complex" (Charkoudian et al. 2015, 7).

Linking the particulars of this case study of the SaLT program back to our conceptual framework, we want to highlight how inviting students from underrepresented and underserved groups in particular to take on the role of student partner aims to redress epistemic, affective, and ontological harms. It redresses epistemic injustice (Fricker 2007) by recognizing those students' expertise, valuing them as knowers and as creators of knowledge (Delgado Bernal 2002), and giving them the epistemic credit they deserve (Kotzee 2017). When underrepresented students are positioned to draw on their lived experiences as forms of knowledge and expertise to inform pedagogical practice and curriculum design and redesign, they can both influence and see immediate changes: in faculty awareness, in pedagogical approach, and in curriculum design. As one student (also quoted in chapter 3) explained: "Participating in the partnerships program makes me feel as though my perspective on education and learning matters"—an experience that, as a Black female, contrasts sharply with other experiences, such as another one we noted in chapter 3: "All too often, when the black girl speaks or tries to offer an intellectual analysis of issues at hand, her perspective is denied or deemed unworthy" (student quoted in Cook-Sather and Seay 2020).

Affirming and responding to students on the affective level and recognizing and supporting, as well as compensating them monetarily for, their time and the emotional work they invest can help redress a variety of affective harms. As one student partner asserted:

[Working in partnership makes] invisible things visible. I know I have been doing a lot of emotional labor here [at the colleges] since the beginning, I know that, I will name that, but it's usually been unrecognized institutionally. . . . [Partnership] makes that work visible. It's paid. And then discussing it in the weekly meetings and feeling like we are all doing this work . . . we're being affirmed in doing this work for the institution and also for each other. (Student partner quoted in Cook-Sather 2018b, 927)

Furthermore, when students are, as one student explained, "working along-side those that are typically viewed as having the power (faculty)," they feel as though they can "create change or make an impact" (student quoted in Cook-Sather and Agu 2013, 277). Their "experiences as a student" are not only "validated" (student quoted in Cook-Sather and Seay 2020) but also build students' sense of self-efficacy, enhance their sense of capacity and competency, and reinforce their personal effectiveness and confidence in making change. All of these stand in stark contrast to the self-doubt, sense of futility, hopelessness, inertia, and powerlessness that characterize the harms so many students experience from the violences of postsecondary education.

Recognizing, positioning, and valuing students as knowers and affirming and responding to the affective aspects of their lived experiences in pedagogical partnership work focused on classroom and curricular experiences work as well to redress ontological harm—when students feel that who they are is negated or prevented. If a student's sense of who they are and who they might become is invalidated or undermined, it interferes with the essential features of personhood and human flourishing: capacity for autonomy, self-determination, and agency (Kahn 2017). The position of pedagogical and curricular consultant, the role of cocreator—positions and roles, as numerous students have indicated, that are not typically open to "people like them" (i.e., from underrepresented groups)—inform their sense of who they are, their capacity, and their agency. The power of their presence—in weekly classroom observations, in regular meetings to redesign curriculum—and the immediate responses they receive to their perspectives and recommendations, which are not only valued but also often directly and immediately inform classroom practice or curricular design and redesign, thereby help to redress some of the ontological harm these students might have experienced. Students who have participated in SaLT have spoken to this potential, asserting that their experiences of pedagogical partnership served to "affirm who I am" (student quoted in Cook-Sather and Agu, 2013, p. 273) and made them feel as though, as the student quoted in chapter 3 asserted, "who I am is more than enough—that my identity, my thoughts, my ideas are significant and valuable" (Cook-Sather and Agu 2013, 277). The invitations, recognition, and valuing students experience through pedagogical partnership can also mobilize an ontological or "culture shift" on postsecondary education campuses by challenging dominant neoliberal ontologies and validating alternative worldviews, further affirming the personhood of students in those partnerships (Cook-Sather et al. 2019).

Although the main focus of pedagogical partnerships through the SaLT program is classroom and curricular exploration and development, extensions of these formal strands of the program also emerge in response to particular circumstances. For instance, after working in a classroom-focused pedagogical partnership with a faculty member, Leslie shifted her focus to research into how pedagogical partnerships can support more equitable and just practices and redress harm. With support from an Arthur Vining Davis Foundations grant through the Pennsylvania Consortium for the Liberal Arts, Leslie both pursued her own research project and took on the role of coresearcher with the rest of the authors of this book (de Bie et al. 2019). Further building on that work, Leslie developed two new projects. The first was an independent study through which she delved more deeply into literature on knowledge creation and critical race theory and met regularly with a visiting professor at Haverford College to explore decolonizing practices in relation to her research and his teaching. This project was a fortuitous linking of a faculty member's pedagogical commitments with one of Leslie's areas of research she took advantage of to further her (and the faculty member's) work.

The second project was the development of a set of resources for all faculty who participate in the SaLT program that includes recommendations generated from Leslie's collaboration with the visiting faculty member and illustrative examples from her own experience and from her research. This project resulted from an inequitable situation in which Leslie found herself: a campus job that had unreliable and unpredictable hours. In conversation with Alison, she decided to leave that job in favor of the opportunity to develop resources for faculty. Like the SaLT program itself, this extension of its resources to support Leslie drawing on her experiences, expertise, and insights contributed to, although certainly did not fully effect, the redress of epistemic, affective, and ontological harms she has experienced. The projects previously described not only allowed Leslie to receive monetary compensation for her work toward equitable classroom practices but also provided her opportunities to advance her passion for research and have her campus job contribute to her graduate school preparation. This extension of the SaLT program as well as the program itself create job opportunities for students that support their academic pursuits and thereby challenge what traditional college jobs look like. (See Leslie's section in chapter 6 for an expanded discussion of this point.)

## Case Study: The Student Partners Program at McMaster University

McMaster University is a medium-sized, medical-doctoral institution in Hamilton, Canada, which enrolls approximately 33,000 students (undergraduate and graduate) annually. The institution defines itself as a "research-intensive, student-centred university dedicated to advancing human and societal health and well-being" (McMaster University n.d., para. 3), and has a long history of being recognized both for research outcomes and pedagogical innovation. In 2013–2014, the university's Student Partners Program (SPP) was developed by the central teaching and learning institute (the Paul R. MacPherson Institute for Leadership, Innovation, and Excellence in Teaching), in partnership with faculty and students from the Arts and Science Program—a small, interdisciplinary liberal arts program on the campus with a focus on inquiry-based and socially engaged learning. Influenced by successful initiatives like the SaLT program and the growing body of research about student–faculty partnerships, its central aims were to support the development of meaningful collaborations among faculty, staff, and students on pedagogical initiatives, in order to enhance teaching and learning on campus and support positive outcomes for participants.

In its first year, the program involved 13 undergraduate students from the Arts and Science program, who partnered primarily with teaching and learning institute staff on projects that included pedagogical research and course design and analysis. Research and evaluation conducted in conjunction with the pilot offering (e.g., Marquis, Puri et al. 2016) demonstrated the program's efficacy and potential, and generated suggestions for refining and enhancing it going forward. Given the findings from this preliminary research, and from subsequent scholarship investigating partnership both within the SPP and beyond (e.g., Marquis, Black, and Healey 2017; Marquis, Power, and Yin 2019; Marquis et al. 2017; Marquis et al. 2018), the program was subsequently refined and expanded, and now engages a range of students, faculty, and staff from across campus (more than 200 per year in recent years).

Projects included in the SPP are selected via open calls, circulated three times per academic year, that invite faculty, staff, and students to submit projects that align with the program goals. Although any type of project that stands to enhance teaching and learning through partnership is eligible for inclusion, the program oversight team has also established specific program streams that aim to support partnerships in different areas of teaching and learning practice. The first (and historically largest) stream focuses primarily on engaging students and faculty and staff as coinquirers on SoTL research projects, but has also included a range of other initiatives such as resource development and opportunities to design and implement cocurricular learning programming or educational development offerings. A second stream partners students and faculty who work together to (re)design courses, or to investigate and refine one of the faculty partner's courses as it is being taught. The final stream of the current program model engages students as partners in curriculum review and quality enhancement processes. In this case, students and faculty work together on developing portions of an academic degree program's internal review documents, or on implementing suggestions and strategies for development generated by the program review process. Student–faculty partnership has also been embedded into a faculty fellowship program supported by the teaching and learning institute, through which students and faculty collaborate on projects focused on evaluating course impact or implementing program change. Regardless of the stream in which they are participating, students are paid for their contributions (with most working approximately 3–5 hours per week for one or more terms). All SPP participants also have access to resources and consultation that might support their projects and are eligible to apply for funding to enable students to copresent their work at conferences and other teaching and learning events.

Beyond its aim to develop and support partnerships that trouble traditional power dynamics and support more egalitarian ways of working, the SPP was not initially focused explicitly on questions of equity in postsecondary education. Similarly, it was not conceived primarily as an opportunity for students who identify as members of equity-seeking groups; rather, it is advertised broadly to all students enrolled at the institution. This, of course, raises questions about who has access to the program, and, indeed, research conducted about the SPP indicates that students with established networks or particular experiences on campus may feel more likely to apply than others (Marquis et al. 2018). Nevertheless, the program has included several projects focused on equity since its outset, and a number of students who identify as members of marginalized and underrepresented groups have participated. In recent years, the SPP team has attempted to develop the program's potential contributions to equity on campus in several ways: by including attention to equity and inclusion in project selection criteria, by reiterating in student calls that the program aims to involve a diverse range of people, by conducting research on the experiences of equity-seeking students taking part in the program (Cook-Sather et al. 2019; de Bie et al. 2019; Marquis et al. forthcoming; Study 2, Appendix A), and by supporting a number of equity-focused projects, that, in some cases, explicitly prioritize hiring student partners who themselves identify as members of marginalized groups (e.g., Brown et al. 2020; de Bie and Brown 2017). Most recently, an equity-focused stream of the SPP, which partners students who occupy one or more marginalized social locations with faculty to work on projects focused specifically on enhancing equity and inclusion in courses and programs, has been developed and piloted (Marquis, Carrasco-Acosta et al. 2019; Woolmer, Marquis et al. 2019). These are only first steps, and continuing to think about means of developing the SPP's potential to contribute to equity in postsecondary education will be important as the program continues to evolve.

Data collected in both research and informal evaluation of the SPP resonate with many of the forms of epistemic, affective, and ontological redress discussed in chapter 3 and in relation to the SaLT program discussed in the preceding paragraphs. Here, we focus in particular on how research-focused pedagogical partnerships such as those conducted through McMaster's SPP have the potential to further articulate the harms discussed in chapter 2, as well as facilitate forms of epistemic, affective, and ontological justice. We describe two specific research projects and consider their potential contributions to equity.

One of these projects, which was supported by the MacPherson Institute teaching fellowship program and involved partnership with two students, occurred within the School of Social Work on campus. The project sought to respond to the concerns of social work students from equity-seeking groups (racialized, Indigenous, 2SLGBTQ, disabled students) with regard to field education experiences—the "practice-focused" part of the social work program where students are placed in a community agency to observe and work with social work professionals and apply social work skills. It involved focus groups, interviews, and surveys with approximately 30 students from these groups, with a focus on analyzing student feedback to determine and act on recommendations for change. Alise was involved in supporting this project as a student partner, and so the analysis that took place was informed by epistemic and affective considerations Alise was already thinking about in relation to their dissertation work and that later came to frame this book. Some of these connections from the "Place-me(a)nt Project," as it came to be called, included explorations of the difficulties that students from equity-seeking groups faced during placement and associated negative impacts on their learning and epistemic pursuits. Students described, for example, being assigned burdensome diversity-related work (e.g., being asked to educate other staff on diversity issues) that they felt interfered with rather than contributed to their learning. Student confidence in their knowledge, skills, and competency was also affected, in some cases, by inadequate or neglectful supervision. The analysis also drew attention to the negative affective states of students from equity-seeking groups in placement—significant worry about facing prejudice and inaccessibility and the additional work of managing these difficult emotions. For a couple of students, this combined lack of epistemic affirmation and support, and distressing emotional components, led to a form of ontological insecurity—questioning whether they could be a social worker (in general, and in certain areas of practice) (see de Bie et al. 2020). Although this research was not expressly focused, theoretically, on epistemic, affective, and ontological harms or redress as such, it does confirm that these types of harm are quite regularly experienced by students across a range of disciplines and curricular experiences and that pedagogical partnership research to further investigate these harms and potential for redress is warranted.

Another recent research project supported by the SPP focused on exploring teaching assistants' (TAs') experiences of teaching in relation to their intersecting social locations and identities. Although the initial intent of this project, which was codesigned by a faculty member (Beth) and two students (Tianna Follwell and Alan Santinele Martino), was to conduct a small number of interviews with undergraduate and graduate TAs, an unexpectedly large number of people volunteered to participate, and the team ultimately ended up interviewing nearly 40 TAs from various disciplines. The project thus provided space for a fairly significant number of people to share experiences that they clearly wanted heard, and drew attention to the epistemic and affective harms (among other things) experienced by some TAs at one Canadian university. For example, several participants occupying marginalized social locations shared stories of having their expertise and knowledge challenged or discounted, described feelings of isolation, and/or recounted experiences in which they felt threatened or had to navigate complex decisions around identity and disclosure during their teaching (Marquis, Santinele Martino, and Follwell 2020). At the same time, some also described bringing their experiences, knowledge, and identities to bear in their teaching in ways that might contribute to equity and justice, for example by foregrounding marginalized perspectives and voices and role-modeling possibilities for being and behaving (Follwell, Santinele Martino, and Marquis 2018). The project thus made clear both the harms that marginalized TAs can experience and the ways in which their efforts, both in the classroom and in sharing their experiences through research, might contribute to enhancing equity both for them and for others. What remains, of course, is to translate this research into concrete initiatives that further recognize and act on these students' experiences and insights.

As these examples illustrate, equity-focused pedagogical research conducted in partnership through programs like the SPP can contribute to the further empirical identification of epistemic, affective, and ontological harms experienced by students from equity-seeking groups, and the exploration of potential forms of redress. Likewise, chapter 3 cited many instances where partnership-based research on student–staff pedagogical partnerships reveals how these partnerships can contribute to the redress of such harms. Here, we further flesh out and nuance some of these possibilities for redress, as well as other mechanisms and domains through which such research-based partnerships can facilitate justice.

First, in relation to epistemic benefits, when students from equity-seeking groups are involved in pedagogical research as partners, they are legitimized as knowers and contributors to theory development and knowledge creation. Partnership research, such as the inquiry conducted in the preparation of this book, can explicitly work to create new theoretical and interpretive resources that expand our capacity to name (in)justice (a hermeneutical form of epistemic justice). Furthermore, contributing to publications or presentations at conferences can offer a kind of epistemic affirmation, as the student quoted in the following excerpt described, that may not be available in the same way during a classroom- or curriculum-focused partnership where knowledge and theory generation is not the goal:

> When I was at conferences and everything, I had people—instructors, for example from [institution name], I remember two particular ladies. They came to me and said—they gave me their card and said—you know, "when you publish this, do send me an email. I need to know more about this." And I was like really impressed. At that time we were at the infancy stage of this project, and I didn't know that people would be that interested. . . . It makes me feel good. . . . And I think it strengthens the feeling of being an effective knowledge translator. (Quoted in Study 2, Appendix A)

Gaining epistemic confidence to share perspectives with faculty or feel assured in one's knowledge is one kind of significant empowerment that is likely to happen across partnership types and scales. However, this is perhaps taken to another level by those who also learn how to navigate academic institutional structures such as academic writing and peer review or who in other ways "go public" with their work beyond the confines of a singular partnership relationship or zone. Instead of seeing "a change in the syllabus" (student quoted in Marquis et al. forthcoming), for example, students may see the possibility for change at a wider scale (e.g., the academic literature in the area) and for enhancing equity for a broader student population via partnership. As one student conducting research through the SPP explained, "This knowledge [produced through research] hopefully is aimed at creating more equitable . . . or . . . inclusive . . . experience in the classroom. That's what we're doing this research for, right?" (quoted in Study 2, Appendix A). These possibilities are not, however, guaranteed. Although classroom and curricular partnership projects have the potential to have an impact on equity whether or not the project takes equity as its focus (because of their broader attention to student learning and experience, as explored in the first case study), this may not always be the case in research-focused partnership projects. Pedagogical research can and often does quite easily avoid issues of equity when, for example, student demographics are not explicitly collected or analyzed in relation to the research question. Corroborating this point, some student coinquirers on research projects supported through the SPP have noted that questions of equity did not really come up during, or feel relevant to, their projects (Study 2, Appendix A).

Second, in relation to affective impacts, pedagogical research conducted in partnership can encourage partners to bring their lived experience, embodied knowledge, and feelings (affect) to all stages of the research—design, research questions, interviews, analysis. In doing so, this type of research can explore ideas otherwise missed by "rational," unemotional, "objective" inquiry. Research as a type of partnership work may also reduce the burden on students to engage in direct emotional and epistemic labor to facilitate change, for example, as happens for those students involved in curriculum review and classroom-based partnerships. The burden of the labor is different, and perhaps at times less encompassing or vulnerability-inducing when students are challenging harm theoretically through a written confrontation with the academic literature instead of in personal conversation with a faculty or staff colleague. Alise has certainly found the labor of writing this book and writing up research papers different from the social navigation of in-person, interactional diversity work.

Third, participating in research may enable particular ontological possibilities for students beyond those of their "student" role. An example we quoted in chapter 3 is of a student coming to feel like a "researcher": "I feel more like I'm an equal partner in the whole structure then, than oh, she's just like the lowly grad student. . . . I guess I'm thinking of myself less as a student and more of just as a researcher" (student quoted in de Bie et al. 2019, 43). Another student wrote: "Reflecting back on the project now, I know that I've developed greatly as a person and scholar—I see the value of my contributions more clearly and feel much more confident" (Black and Guitman 2018). At a research-intensive university like McMaster, coming to participate in research as a true "partner," rather than as a research assistant, may help affirm students as valued contributors to the research mission of the university and open up the ontological possibility for students to begin identifying as scholars. Other types of partnership projects may enable additional valued identities, but these are less likely to be in the "researcher" category. Of course, research-focused partnerships also entail particular challenges and face specific barriers to realizing epistemic, affective, and ontological forms of justice. We discuss these tensions, as well as additional challenges affecting partnership programs including SaLT and the SPP, in the next chapter.

## Conclusion

In addition to describing in more granular detail how different partnership models might work, we hope the preceding case studies also begin to show how the possibilities we explored in chapter 3 may manifest differently depending on specific partnership goals and context. We encourage readers to consider how epistemic, affective, and ontological benefits may (or may not) play out in their own local contexts, and the specific areas of tension that merit thoughtfulness and care. What we have not explored here are how these different partnership possibilities and contexts are also affected by different student identities. Certainly the experiences of students from different equity-seeking groups are not the same. Therefore, the potential benefits of partnership, as well as its risks, are best understood when attentive to these aspects of context and particular dimensions of identity and experience.

Classroom, curricular, research, and programmatic partnerships all have an important role to play in further validating and expanding the conceptual framework presented in this book. Research might more explicitly investigate epistemic, affective, and ontological harms that partnership work has the potential to redress in varying contexts and in relation to different models of working in partnership. Moreover, further attention to challenges and limitations of partnership work, considered in relation to our conceptual framework, is merited. Although we did not attend to such challenges in detail here, we by no means intend to suggest that the case studies presented are exempt from tensions and limitations. Instead, we turn to such challenges in detail in chapter 5, noting that they apply to the kinds of examples discussed in this chapter and arguing that they are likewise worth considering for other programs and initiatives aiming to contribute to equity and justice through pedagogical partnership.

# 5

# TENSIONS IN AND LIMITATIONS OF REDRESSING HARMS THROUGH PARTNERSHIP

Although partnerships have the potential to redress epistemic, affective, and ontological forms of violence and the harms to students that result, and thereby contribute to greater equity, and while evidence suggests these possibilities are being realized in many instances, there remain significant tensions that merit consideration. These tensions include the very real ways that partnerships may unintentionally contribute to the harms we want to avoid and the factors that could get in the way of justice occurring through partnership. In the following, we unpack these tensions in relation to epistemic, affective, and ontological dimensions of experience and, as we do so, invite consideration of whether and how these tensions are evident in our case studies in chapter 4. After our discussion of each tension, we offer recommendations for how to avoid contributing unintentionally to harms and how to tackle barriers to justice through partnership. As is the case throughout this book, we focus our discussion here on challenges and tensions related to the harms equity-seeking students experience, though some of these may also be relevant to faculty and staff belonging to equity-seeking groups, and such faculty and staff may also navigate other challenges and tensions in partnership that require attention (Marquis, Guitman et al. 2020). To confirm whether and how the student-specific impacts we note at the level of individuals and interpersonal relationships translate more broadly to other relationships and systems, further research is required. We return to these questions at the end of this chapter.

## Tensions in Redressing Epistemic Harms Through Partnership

As we noted in chapter 3, recognition of students as knowers can be a powerful thing, but it is not always straightforward, guaranteed, or lasting, given the entrenchment of epistemic violence in postsecondary education, and it may not be enough to repair epistemic harm. Consequently, several epistemic tensions arise, including two that have been explored in previous scholarship and that our analysis affirms and extends—equitable access to partnership and equitable benefit from project outputs—and one that is less well explored and that our analysis further illuminates—epistemic uncertainty and doubt.

### Equitable Access to Partnership

Students from equity-seeking groups may not experience equitable access to partnership, particularly when it takes place within extracurricular programs (Bovill et al. 2016; Felten et al. 2013; Mercer-Mapstone, Islam, and Reid 2021; Moore-Cherry et al. 2016). As Marquis et al. (2018) and Marquis, Jayaratnam et al. (2019) have observed, the process for obtaining a partnership position can be perceived to be competitive, awareness about opportunities can be limited, and students who already have particular kinds of experiences, networks, and social capital may feel more confident in applying than do others. Some positions may also be targeted at students with specific preexisting skills, such as those with relevant research experience for the project, or students might suspect such preexisting skills or experiences are necessary. Given the limited availability of partnership positions, and the uneven intentionality around recruiting students with access to fewer opportunities, it appears likely that some students who apply to partnership positions may already experience relative epistemic confidence. It is possible, then, that many students who have been epistemically marginalized or who have experienced epistemic harms face significant barriers to applying in the first place. Consequently, while partnerships can bolster epistemic confidence and affirm the knowledge of marginalized students, the barriers these students face in accessing partnership opportunities may, in some circumstances, make the likelihood of realizing these benefits relatively low.

### Equitable Benefit From Project Outputs

Another potential tension relates to recognition of a student's contributions over time. For example, the presence or absence of payment for students' work in partnership, as well as the rate of payment (comparative to other pay scales on campus), can have epistemic consequences. If students are not being paid, for example, or feel that they are being underpaid for the intellectual contributions they make to their partnership project, this may be experienced as a form of epistemic disrespect. Even with competitive payment, requesting that students from equity-seeking groups contribute to the redress of systemic oppression they face can still contribute to epistemic exploitation, especially if the burden and difficulty of this work remains underrecognized and it benefits the institution and those with relative privilege more than students from equity-seeking groups (Mercer-Mapstone, Islam, and Reid 2021). In such cases, partnerships involving students from equity-seeking groups might be read as examples of "cultural taxation" (Joseph and Hirshfield 2011, 121; see also James 2012), creating additional responsibilities for marginalized students, relative to their nonmarginalized peers, that benefit the institution more than those directly involved. This inequity can be exacerbated further for students who need to work, because they might not be able to choose to leave a position that feels exploitative.

If caution does not guide the recognition and translation phase of partnership work, it is possible for students in general, and students from equity-seeking groups in particular, to be epistemically marginalized. This is a particular danger if contribution within dominant academic knowledge systems is prioritized over methods that share findings back with a student's communities of affiliation. In such cases, students' epistemic labor may serve others, but not themselves or equity-seeking groups (Pohlhaus 2017). Mercer-Mapstone, Dvorakova, Matthews et al. (2017), for example, have noted how peer-reviewed partnership publications are more often authored or coauthored by faculty and staff partners than by students (despite numerous exceptions), and Woolmer has argued (on a conference panel) that this form of knowledge translation is likely to be more beneficial to an academic's career trajectory than to that of many student partners (Woolmer, Bovill et al. 2019). Student partner projects or contracts may also be relatively short term (Bell, Barahona, and Stanway 2020) and so students may not have the opportunity to be paid to work on a project up until the point of successful publication. Furthermore, producing pedagogical research in partnership does not automatically result in greater equity if those research results are not well disseminated and applied. Therefore, although the research has potential to support wider change, these changes are not guaranteed and may not make their way to having wider redress. As a student partner on a research-focused project explained, "It's hard to know, right, like the actual effect of research" (quoted in Study 2, Appendix A).

Additionally, although students may feel respected within their partnership relationships or teams, this is not necessarily the case when "going public" through publication or sharing insights from partnership work at less receptive academic conferences, as Mathrani (2018), a student partner has described:

> I recently attended an inclusive science teaching workshop at an International Biology conference. The workshop was designed for faculty and post-doctoral students, but given my interest in inclusive science teaching, I decided to attend the workshop. During the interactive workshop, I was at a table with post-doctoral students and faculty members who were thinking about how to make their classes more inclusive. Once we all introduced ourselves at the table, the four people at my table immediately dismissed my presence, talked across me, and did not really allow me the chance to speak. (5–6)

Likewise, while it has the potential to affirm affective knowledge as legitimate and meaningful, research also has a history of invalidating ways of knowing through emotions and embodied experiences; things that might be framed as "personal" are often deemed "inappropriate" to scholarly research and communication (Yahlnaaw 2019)—and may thus be removed (e.g., due to habit or journal requirements) during academic writing or received poorly during the peer-review process.

Alongside these cautions and sites of potential epistemic harm, however, are also examples of student partners presenting and authoring work without faculty (e.g., Mercer-Mapstone, Guitman, and Acai 2019; Ntem 2017), or asserting themselves in academic spaces, such as conferences, where they are not explicitly welcome, as Mathrani (2018) did in response to the dismissal described previously. This suggests the importance of ensuring that research projects do not reinforce epistemic marginalization during the dissemination process. One way to address this is to consider the genre in which writing is produced. Reflective forms of writing, for instance, are more accessible to both readers and writers (Cook-Sather, Abbot, and Felten 2019) and can make space for kinds of expression not typically welcomed in other genres (Cook-Sather, Abbot, and Felten 2019; Healey, Matthews, and Cook-Sather, 2020).

## Epistemic Uncertainty, Doubt, and Marginalization

The nature of partnership across power relations is that students often enter these relationships from a historically marginalized position, which has led many—if not most—students to articulate epistemic uncertainty and self-doubt at the outset of partnership. Indeed, such doubt is one of the threshold concepts to partnership that Cook-Sather, Bahti, and Ntem (2019) identify.

These uncertainties can be related to students' institutional roles (as students), their internalized sense that their knowledge is not valid or legitimate, their lack of subject-matter expertise, their sociocultural identities or locations, and their pedagogical knowledge. Although this is a common theme across partnerships, the impacts can be especially pronounced for students from equity-seeking groups, who may find their uncertainty in a new experience compounded by historical experiences of epistemic injustice and violence. For example, as explored in chapter 2, students from equity-seeking groups may have internalized a range of negative messages about themselves—that they are stupid, incapable, lacking ability. These beliefs may be especially marked at the beginning of a new experience where the self-doubt minoritized students face in the academy is exacerbated by the newness of a partnership role and its invitation to claim expertise and contribute actively to knowledge development and exchange. (See Lorenzo 2020 for a discussion of this point.)

Although it is difficult to correlate reasons for epistemic uncertainty with particular sources, students from equity-seeking groups have often articulated perspectives such as this one from a student partner who identified as female and was underrepresented in the discipline for which she worked as a student partner: "At first I was kind of skeptical because you are a student and these profs have been doing this for quite some time. They have advanced degrees, you're a kid with some college . . . you could easily be dismissed" (student quoted in Cook-Sather and Agu 2013, 280). It may be that when students doubt their capacity because they are "just a student" (Cook-Sather, Bahti, and Ntem 2019), there are other dimensions of their identities at play in their self-doubt. Students from equity-seeking groups have also described instances of having their knowledge explicitly discounted due to their student status or social location, or finding it difficult to challenge the epistemic authority of privileged instructors:

> How do you tell a white male professor who's straight . . . how this works when he is supposed to be the cognitive authority of the class and of his syllabus and all these things. . . . I remember that being very hard but something we talked a lot about. (Student quoted in Marquis et al. forthcoming)

Other times student partners have framed the challenge as needing to "unlearn" internalized conceptions that their knowledge is not valuable. One student described this relation to racialization specifically, for instance, noting, "I think with being a member of a racialized group it comes with a lot of second guessing" (quoted in Study 2, Appendix A). Although some students have argued that partnership can begin to help redress such uncertainty, the following quotation makes clear that this process may be difficult and partial:

> I still have uncertainties about contributing ideas and whether what I have to say is of value or not, but being in a partnership has definitely helped me understand that I can say things and have them be listened to by faculty and staff, which is something I never really thought could happen. (Student quoted in Cook-Sather et al. 2019, 27)

As another specific site of epistemic uncertainty, pedagogical research can be incredibly difficult and overwhelming for students from equity-seeking groups engaging in these activities for the first time. Doing so through a partnership, though, can mediate some of this uncertainty by creating a space for trying new things without fear of failure—a safety net that may not exist in other research relations. Such possibilities are reflected in the following quotation, from a story about one of the research partnerships described in chapter 4: "As an undergraduate, Tianna has often thought, 'wow, thank god I can make mistakes here,' while Alan noted that feelings of safety allowed him to try new things and make meaningful contributions" (Michell 2019).

In some cases, partnerships might also not succeed in recognizing or valuing students' epistemic contributions. Ntem and Cook-Sather (2018), for instance, documented several cases in which faculty partners appeared to student partners to demonstrate resistance to students' knowledge and ideas. Likewise, epistemic marginalization can result inadvertently, when individuals participating in partnership are not aware of the situatedness of their knowledge and assume the necessity, correctness, or universality of particular socially constructed ways of knowing and being. Yahlnaaw (2019) has described such an experience of epistemic marginalization:

> I was invited to collaborate in a session. In the planning process, my approach to research was labelled "alternative" because I do not believe in data collection in the Western tradition. Indigenous knowledges were present long before colonial knowledges; therefore, if anything is to be labelled alternative, it is colonial knowledges because they came after. At first, this left my colleagues with blank stares which soon transitioned into what appeared to be pure shock, realization, and understanding of what I was trying to articulate to them. (7)

Given this and other experiences, Yahlnaaw (2019) argued that partnership is "often tokenistic" despite being "fostered by good intentions" (7) and asked "how does the taken for granted dominance of colonial ways of knowing and being" in the academy and in particular scholarly organizations "create space for Indigenous people, either students or faculty, to be partners in learning and teaching?" (7–8).

Although these forms of epistemic doubt, dismissal, or difficulty can impede the realization of epistemic justice, and carry the possibility of causing particular harm to student partners from equity-seeking groups, throughout the life of a partnership many students do move through doubts and difficulty into greater epistemic confidence or, as indicated in the quotation from Yahlnaaw (2019), assert and affirm their knowledge in the face of its potential erasure or marginalization. To facilitate this movement and epistemic affirmation, and to support students encountering marginalization or resistance, it is important for students to have opportunities to talk through their experiences, such as in the context of regular meetings with other student partners.

### Recommendations for Mediating Unintentional Contributions to Epistemic Harms and Barriers to Justice

Given the epistemic tensions that have been discussed, it is important to consider what can maximize the likelihood of epistemic justice and most effectively challenge and redress epistemic harm during partnership work and associated knowledge dissemination. In order to mediate and reduce possibilities for epistemic harm, our recommended strategies include:

- practicing intentionality with recruitment processes and encouraging and supporting students from historically marginalized groups in applying for partnership positions (Bovill et al. 2016; Mercer-Mapstone, Islam, and Reid 2021);
- thoughtfully considering issues of recognition and compensation in partnership so that students feel respected and fairly acknowledged for their contributions;
- being transparent about how epistemic uncertainty and doubt are very common experiences, especially at the beginning of partnership;
- offering ongoing support to students from equity-seeking groups involved in partnership—especially opportunities that affirm students' knowledge, create a cohort effect, and help students feel less alone;
- providing explicit feedback and affirmation to counter negative messages students may have internalized about their abilities;
- having explicit conversations about "dissemination" of insights and findings and facilitating such opportunities students find most beneficial;

- seeking to create welcoming and inclusive teaching and learning conferences that invite the participation of students or opportunities for students to design and facilitate their own workshops for faculty and staff on their home campuses; and
- pursuing publication in venues that acknowledge the value of partnership and support principles such as methodological and epistemological pluralism.

Additionally, although there is evidence that students do and can gain epistemic confidence from their work in partnership, we have only anecdotal evidence for how long it takes for students to experience this benefit and regarding what factors might make this more or less possible. Although we have witnessed and experienced such gaining of confidence within several weeks and certainly within single semesters, we have also seen and experienced such confidence shaken and undermined (Ntem and Cook-Sather 2018). Therefore, further research in this area is warranted to explore this phenomenon across contexts and partner styles and approaches as well as over time.

## Tensions in Redressing Affective Harms Through Partnership

Although partnership has the potential to contribute to affective forms of redress from injustice, it is also the case that partnership can be emotionally complex and demanding. One noted limitation of partnership literature is that it appears to underreport negative experiences of partnership (Healey et al. 2019; Mercer-Mapstone, Dvorakova, Matthews et al. 2017), and so the affective possibilities of partnership that we highlight in this book may not be shared by all students, especially those who have not participated in the available research we cite. It is thus important to research and identify areas where students may not universally share positive experiences, and may in fact experience difficult and detrimental emotions. We take up the following range of emotional complexities here: emotional labor, challenges of belonging, and potentially alienating affective norms.

### Emotional Labor

As we indicated in chapter 3, although many people have written about the challenges of navigating power differentials in partnerships (Bovill et al. 2016; Felten 2017; Marquis, Black, and Healey 2017; Marquis, Puri et al. 2016; Ntem and Cook-Sather 2018; Seale et al. 2015; Verwoord and Smith 2020), these are not always considered extensively in relation to affect or equity. More often, as also noted in chapter 3, they are addressed in terms of mitigating power differentials and creating more egalitarian relationships. When we bring an equity frame to power-related challenges, however, as we do with the framework we present in this book, the affective dimensions of working against institutionalized power differences are made apparent. As such, while partnerships can sometimes support and enable *relief* from emotional labor within inequitable institutions that reinforce structural disadvantages, they may also be seen as demanding particular kinds of emotion work (Cook-Sather, Bahti, and Ntem 2019). This may be especially the case when equity-seeking students partner with faculty who occupy privileged social locations and endeavor to contribute to more equitable classrooms. As one of the student participants in Ntem and Cook-Sather's (2018) study described,

> We've seen in the [student partner] meetings how emotionally vulnerable some of my peers are willing to be in our partnerships in order to think about justice [and] racial or gender equality. It's very moving to see my peers give themselves so much, give so much of themselves in their partnerships to make professors understand, to give professors perspective on their experience. (92)

Although such emotional vulnerability can be moving and empowering some times and for some students, it can also become too much. For instance, a student from an underrepresented group at one of our campuses who had alluded in the weekly student partner meetings to the epistemic, affective, and ontological violence and resulting harms she had experienced at the college was working with a faculty member from a well-represented group. In a discussion at one of those weekly meetings regarding the extent to which she should document and share with her faculty partner her previous experiences of harm to try to help him move toward more equitable and just practices, this student partner indicated that doing that kind of reflection and documentation would in fact further and deepen the harm she had experienced. She and Alison therefore decided that she should not take that approach.

Ntem and Cook-Sather (2018) have documented a different kind of emotion work that partnership can demand: navigating experiences of perceived resistance, which are sometimes reported by student partners from equity-seeking groups. For one group of student partners such perceived resistances took the form of inaccurate views faculty seemed to have of students' behavior and capacities. These views seemed to apply both to students enrolled in these faculty members' courses and to student partners. Student partners also perceived an associated refusal to trust and engage them in certain ways. Finally, they discerned faculty fears regarding student–faculty relationships, institutional pressures, and changing established pedagogical habits and associated distancing from these relationships, pressures, and habits. From the students' perspective, all of these forms of resistance got in the way of building productive partnerships. In response, student partners developed strategies to manage these perceived resistances, including endeavoring to (re)build trust and relationship, "leaning in" to whatever form of resistance they perceived by continuing to try to connect with their faculty partners, and stepping back or letting go out of self-protection (Ntem and Cook-Sather 2018). All of these took an emotional toll, however, and the weekly student partner meetings proved vital to supporting students in managing that emotional labor.

## Challenges of Belonging

The notion of belonging described as a potential positive effect in chapter 3 also merits further consideration in relation to underlying tensions. There are many barriers to student partners feeling a sense of belonging through partnership. For example, they may not feel welcome to bring their whole self into partnership (Colón García 2017; Yahlnaaw 2019) or comfortable disclosing their marginalized identities, and consequently feel isolated and like they have to restrict or compromise part of who they are. Even when participating in partnership affirms and responds to students' humanity and fosters belonging *within* partnership, this sense of affirmation and belonging does not necessarily carry into wider contexts:

> I feel that participating in the partnership made me feel more connected to other student consultants, and to faculty and professors. I felt a strong sense of community and trust with other consultants because of the kind of work we were involved in (work that requires you to be very open and honest), and I felt connected to more faculty and professors because I had renewed appreciation for their effort and creativity. However, I don't think it made me feel an increased sense of belonging on a campus wide scale. (Student quoted in Study 3, Appendix A; see also partial quote in Cook-Sather and Seay 2020)

Students may also experience difficulty moving from an affirming environment of partnership back to the typical violence and neglect in other aspects of their life as a student. Seeing and experiencing a viable alternative way of relating through partnership may bring into stark contrast the typical operations of the academy, thereby aggravating loneliness and distress (de Bie 2020; de Bie and Raaper 2019). One student reflected:

> It can be difficult to have a realm . . . where you feel incredibly empowered and your voice is valued, and others where it is not. It can create frustrations when you feel as though in certain arenas your voice is valued and invited, and in others you may just have to sit back and grit your teeth some because your feedback is not invited or may be clearly unwelcome. (Cook-Sather and Alter 2011, 48)

Partnerships may then facilitate affective redress on a local or individual scale—such as a greater sense of belonging—while failing to change systemic structures and make institutions more widely inclusive. It is also possible that when we encourage belonging, we are inviting students to belong to historically violent institutions, or acculturating students into the academy as opposed to radically shifting existing structures (Gibson 2015; Vermette 2012). We may be asking students to assume some complicity as "insiders" within the institution, rather than supporting a politicized refusal to belong or otherwise assimilate into exclusionary academic norms. Moreover, as we elaborate in the following section, when the process of acculturation entails developing empathy for faculty, this may contribute to the dampening of student resistance and opposition to the institution, as well as an emphasis on interpersonal dialogue or incremental tinkering rather than transformative change (de Bie 2020).

## Potentially Alienating Affective Norms

Partnership spaces—especially those that form at a large and formal scale (conferences, publications)—can, like other communities, come to foster and maintain an affective "norm" that isolates those who experience a different range of affects than those that others appear to share. As Alise has written,

> The discussion of emotions—especially negative ones—in the SaP literature is problematically sparse (Felten 2017; Mercer-Mapstone, Dvorakova, Matthews et al. 2017), which can pressure participants to put an idealistic spin on their experiences, as Mercer-Mapstone et al. ("Idealism," 2017, p. 6) have described:
>
> > "We each aspired to achieve the positive aspects of partnership without leaving space for the nitty-gritty messiness. . . . For us, this meant being friendly, supportive, respectful, polite, diplomatic—nice. . . . We unintentionally left no space for conflict." (de Bie, 2020, p. 6)

Those who do not "feel" as they are supposed to—cheerful, hopeful, proud, energized, like they belong—can come to feel excluded and suppress their divergent affective responses. In such a space, students from equity-seeking groups who feel tremendous anger at the violence of the academy, doubt in their abilities, suspicion over the possibilities of partnership (Elaneh 2019), or despair, frustration, and exhaustion in making change may feel unable to share or have heard these varied emotions. This matters for all of us, but perhaps especially for students from equity-seeking groups who may be more likely to experience difficult emotions given the violence they disproportionately face from the institution at large.

Students from equity-seeking groups may face challenges in negotiating multiple knowledge systems and sets of values, politics, and ethics from their social movements and communities of affiliation within partnership spaces. For example, as described by de Bie (2020) and de Bie and Raaper (2019), principles of partnership focused on trust may not mesh with a community politics of distrusting partnership. Such a politics of suspicion is common within psychiatric survivor movements, for example, where partnership between service users and service providers, and between survivors and academics, have been contentious for many years (de Bie 2020). Students from equity-seeking groups may thus face forms of confusion and dissonance in negotiating partnership spaces—at epistemic and ontological levels, perhaps, but also as an additional form of emotional labor.

Relatedly, one of the often identified and celebrated outcomes of partnership is the empathy that student, staff, and faculty partners develop for each other through their work (Cook-Sather and Mejia 2018; Ntem 2020). Although empathy can no doubt contribute to various forms of redress and greater equity, less discussed is how the establishment of empathy and solidarity between faculty and students could also potentially mitigate efforts for social change by, for example, discouraging equity-seeking students from engaging in resistance or critique (de Bie 2020; de Bie and Raaper 2019). In this case, an uncritical encouragement toward "empathy" advanced by partnership literature may be negatively impacting the possibilities of partnership to enhance equity in some circumstances. Patton et al. (2019) have also raised the critique of how campus diversity initiatives often focus on microlevel "interactions and cross-cultural relationships" among diverse groups, "which may certainly benefit individual people, but does little to shift systems" (187). We might similarly be concerned by the degree to which celebrated affective experiences like increased empathy between student and faculty partners enable, facilitate, impede, or fail to support systemic forms of change, or whether and how the "benefit" of increased empathy is experienced by differently situated participants. Who benefits most from dialoguing across difference?

### Recommendations for Mediating Unintentional Contributions to Affective Harms and Barriers to Justice

Taken together, then, these considerations suggest that although partnership has the potential to facilitate affective forms of justice, such redress is not guaranteed. As such, to maximize partnership's potential contributions to equity, it is imperative to acknowledge the tensions that can constitute barriers or limitations to affective redress and the ways in which partnership might itself precipitate emotional harms in some cases, and to proactively attempt to mitigate such harms. Our recommendations include:

- naming emotional labor as such, supporting student partners to carefully consider the possibilities and harms of this work, and encouraging student partners to set limits and make choices that prioritize their well-being, including when that means stepping back from certain forms of engagement in the partnership work, as described in Ntem and Cook-Sather (2018);
- explicitly naming phenomena such as achieving a sense of belonging at the expense of certain dimensions of one's identity, and making these topics of discussion between student and faculty partners (as possible and helpful), at regular meetings of student partners (as an ongoing commitment), and in publications (as in Colón García 2017 and Perez-Putnam 2016);
- recognizing the responsibilities of staff and faculty to student partners beyond the scope of the partnership—such as in difficulties of shifting between partnership and hierarchical, oppressive spaces, and making discussion of such shifts and transitions an intentional part of the work, as in regular meetings of student partners in some contexts (Cook-Sather, Bahti, and Ntem 2019; Woolmer, Bovill et al. 2019);
- encouraging and increasing the publication of "negative" outcomes and experiences of partnership (Mercer-Mapstone, Dvorakova, Matthews, Cook-Sather, and Healey 2017); and
- creating space for expressing unpopular and dissonant affective experiences and affirming these as valid and important, both to support those students experiencing them and to deepen all partners' awareness of the range of affective dimensions of partnership work.

## Tensions in Redressing Ontological Harms Through Partnership

Partnerships focused on enhancing equity can also raise a range of ontological tensions, including those related to partnership language, suppression of full selves, and the difficulty of agency.

## Partnership Language

The language used to refer to people working in partnership has been critiqued on a number of fronts for constraining roles and possibilities for being. Although we are not the first to highlight the importance of considering the language we use to name partners and partnership practices in order to avoid undermining the espoused premises of partnership (Cook-Sather, Bahti, and Ntem 2019; Cook-Sather, Bovill, and Felten 2014; Cook-Sather et al. 2018; Healey et al. 2019), we focus here on the ontological ramifications of these language choices, a lens frequently underlying but typically not explicitly adopted in prior writing.

The term *students as partners* is increasingly used as "an umbrella term" (Matthews et al. 2018, 25) to refer to the community of practitioners and scholars committed to working together through partnership in postsecondary education (Cook-Sather et al. 2018). Striving to name students as colleagues, as producers of knowledge (Neary 2010) rather than passive consumers of it (Ramsden 2008), the term *students as partners* first emerged in the United Kingdom "as part of a counter discourse to Student Engagement policy drives" (Cook-Sather, Matthews et al. 2018, 2) and in the United States in reference to course redesign projects (Mihans, Long, and Felten 2008), in both cases to offer an alternative to more traditional hierarchical relationships (Cook-Sather et al. 2018). Other terms for this work that name both participants (i.e., *student–staff partnership* and *student–faculty partnership*) and terms that name neither (i.e., *cocreating learning and teaching* as in Bovill, Cook-Sather, and Felten 2011) strive for greater equity by not assuming that only one group (students) needs naming (Cook-Sather et al. 2018).

The original impetus behind the creation of the terms *partnership* and *students as partners* was toward greater equity and justice for students as knowers and people. And yet, in addition to the complexities noted previously, the terms do not mean the same thing to everyone across contexts (Cook-Sather et al. 2018; Green 2019). For instance, *partners* in Germany and the Netherlands is likely to evoke sexual partners and in France *partnership* evokes business relationships (Cook-Sather et al. 2018). In Aotearoa/New Zealand, the term *partnership* can signal disenfranchisement by evoking what many Māori experience as failed promises made by the British Crown traced back to the Treaty of Waitangi, the founding document of the country (Cook-Sather 2018c), even though the premises of partnership we discuss here are closely aligned with many Māori values (Lenihan-Ikin et al. 2020; Leota and Sutherland 2020). Relatedly, in Western medical systems with "patient engagement" directives, service users may associate *partnership* (and related terms, such as *engagement* and *involvement*) with public policy statements that rhetorically endorse partnership but do not fulfill its principles in practice (de Bie 2020). Regardless of the terms' intent, then, *partnership*, like *students as partners*, can be misunderstood, evoking reactions and associations that are not shared.

The term *students as partners* in particular can also be misappropriated to describe a consumerist, neoliberal approach to student engagement (Dwyer 2018; Healey and Healey 2018; Healey, Healey, and Cliffe 2018; Matthews, Dwyer et al. 2019; Woolmer 2018)—using partnership language to refer to student satisfaction and education as a product as opposed to engaging in the reciprocal process of partnership. When the term is used to refer to practices more in keeping with consumerism (e.g., the profile and ranking of the university), this constitutes a misappropriation and undercuts the possibility of realizing different ways of being in the process.

Some student partners find the term especially problematic because it signals that they (students) are not doing the naming, and thereby lack agency and authority (Cook-Sather et al. 2018). Some also feel that the term is tokenistic (Yahlnaaw 2019), assumes their sense of self as a partner is defined by their relationship to faculty or staff, and fails to represent the complexities (of experience and identity) they bring to partnership. These critiques suggest that there may be ontological troubles with the language of partnership itself:

> [N]aming only one participant in the term "students as partners" assumes academics/faculty, or staff more broadly, do not need to be named. Thus, by mentioning only students, the term can be at odds with the principles of reciprocity that define the notion of partnership (Cook-Sather, Bovill, and Felten, 2014; Cook-Sather and Felten, 2017) and are central to power sharing in partnership praxis (Matthews, 2017). Furthermore, as *IJSaP* [*International Journal for Students as Partners*] student co-editor Rachel Guitman notes, in naming only students, the term lends itself to tokenistic inclusion of students and generally tokenistic understandings of the practices the term aims to signal (personal communication, August 12, 2018). (Cook-Sather et al. 2018, 3–4)

Given the language politics within disability communities, disabled students may find the language of *student as partner* euphemistic, patronizing, and echoing "politically correct" person-first language (e.g., person with a disability) as opposed to the politicized identity-first language (e.g., disabled person) often preferred by disability activists (de Bie 2020). Consequently, for someone who has lost a sense of self through violence, becoming a student partner may present a new selfhood of "who they can be," but it can be a limiting one that restricts imagination of other roles. A "partner" identity is also a temporary or added-on identity as opposed to a more integrated one that will carry on after a partnership relationship or project has ended. We may thus need alternative, more flexible terms in some cases to open up ontological possibilities for students involved in partnership work.

Another language-related question has to do with the language used not only about but also within partnership work. What terms might student and faculty partners, and program directors or facilitators of partnership work, use to communicate with one another? As Cook-Sather, Bovill, and Felten (2014) have argued, it is certainly important to avoid phrases such as "'giving students voice' and 'using' students as consultants . . . [that] . . . convey a message that students have voice only when . . . faculty bestow it upon them and that students are a means to an end" (136). A question to ask, then, is how the language used within partnership work either exacerbates or works to redress epistemic, affective, and ontological harms students experience. Although we have emphasized some of the ontological implications here, the language we use can simultaneously impact students at epistemic and affective levels (e.g., recognition as knowers, sense of belonging).

Beyond the language about partnership and partners, all other language we use within partnerships is meaningful and has implications for epistemic, affective, ontological justice. For example, the terms we use to talk about equity and justice require careful consideration. Bloch-Schulman (in Wilson et al. 2020) has pointed out that the language of equality and equity within pedagogical partnership writing may "point in the right direction but remain open to multiple interpretations" (54). He therefore encourages further consideration of the use of these terms, such as "what these terms might mean and why we highlight certain meanings over others" (Bloch-Shulman, in Wilson et al. 2020, 54). We make a similar case in chapter 1 and throughout this book in our adoption of the language of equity, justice, violence, and harm.

## Suppression of Full Selves

Student partners may not feel able to be their full selves within partnerships—when their partnership work seems to require them to enact different values than some of their other commitments, when partnership fails to dismantle Eurocentric academic ontologies or invites students to adopt a culturally dissonant way of being, and when going public with partnership work.

Some—perhaps many, or all—students feel unable to bring their full selves to partnership work, at least in some cases and contexts. Yahlnaaw

(2019) has articulated the need for ontological recognition directly, noting, "I want to engage in partnerships where I can bring myself and be myself"—possibilities that had not always been realized in their previous partnership work (8). Other students have shared similar experiences. For example, as we noted in chapter 3, Colón García (2017) described how she adapted to a faculty partner's communication style and "didn't feel as fully welcomed for [her] whole self as [she] had in [her] first partnership" (3). Likewise, the student partner we quoted in chapter 3 who described feeling like they sometimes "lose a part of [themselves]" so others are able to share *their* full selves elaborated:

> I think one thing I am realizing about myself recently, which I think is from identifying as an . . . Asian-American woman, is that I am really slow to speak, and I often listen, but it's like listening to a fault and then internally processing everything because I don't want to offend anyone. I take on a facilitator perspective. I want everyone to feel comfortable sharing their stuff, then I lose a part of myself so they feel safe around me to share their full selves. So that's been tricky. Because as I am translating between them I am trying to figure out where do I go. How do I care for me in that? I think, "Wow, that is offensive to me but I am here to listen to you." (Student quoted in Marquis et al. forthcoming)

These examples, like some of the stories of navigating faculty resistance described previously in relation to emotional labor, make clear that partnership may not always successfully recognize and affirm students' identities and ways of being.

Another way in which students may feel the need to suppress their full selves is when their partnership work seems to require them to enact different values from some of their other commitments. Students, especially those from equity-seeking groups, may wrestle with the ontological complexities of becoming more entrenched in postsecondary institutional structures through partnership, which offers a kind of belonging but may also cause students to feel like they are becoming part of the problem of the institution and/or are in conflict with social movement commitments to oppose the institution. They may feel restricted or like they have to compromise in partnership projects—like they have to find a way to work within the system instead of outside of it. Related constraints have led some to initiate projects aligned with subversive partnership philosophies outside of the academy rather than within it (Neary 2016; Neary and Saunders 2016).

Additionally, partnership might be seen as a Western or Eurocentric remedy to the problem of hierarchical, nondemocratic relationships in postsecondary education, which are themselves framed in relation to, and produced by, Western thought and practices (Marquis et al. forthcoming)—and thereby fail to dismantle Eurocentric ontologies on which the academy is based. For students identifying with non-Western cultural traditions, partnership can thus be especially challenging and encourage students to enact a culturally dissonant self, as suggested by a student who noted that partnership "started out as very uncomfortable for [them] because [they] grew up in a culture that emphasizes respecting your elders and upholding the hierarchy" (student quoted in Marquis et al. forthcoming; see also Lorenzo 2020 and Seow 2019). Writing in Malaysia, another student offered a similar perspective:

> When Dr. Amrita invited me to provide feedback on the "Learning and Individual Differences" course she had taught for a long time, I was both excited and hesitant about the opportunity. I was hesitant because the invitation was unusual and sounded quite radical to me, since it is not something common in our culture. Despite this, I decided to take up the challenge. . . . The traditional concept of faculty and student's relationship is hierarchical, formal, and rigid. The faculty could be friendly but never be friends with a student. They teach, guide, facilitate, comment, correct, and are accountable for students' academic performance, but students cannot take on those roles for faculty. Even though we understand that teachers have certain limitations, Malaysian students generally view teachers or lecturers as people who have the authority and are the knowledge bearers. We are taught at a young age to show respect, listen, and obey, rather than question them. So, questioning or disagreeing with your teachers is a "no no." Our curiosity or need to question must be restrained and reframed on most occasions. Therefore, my brain automatically began to generate numerous thoughts! Why? Why me? I have no formal teaching experience; I am inexperienced, what is there that I could contribute to her teaching? Will she value my comments as constructive, or will she give me a frown? (Kaur and Yong Bing 2020, 63)

Although some student partners ultimately come to argue that they value learning about and being in these new kinds of relationship, it is worth considering the extent to which partnership practices assume or require Eurocentric models of respect and reciprocity and marginalize other ways of realizing these values in the process (Marquis et al. forthcoming).

Likewise, it is essential to consider how partnership might reflect, rather than challenge, "the taken-for-granted dominance of colonial ways of knowing and being" more broadly (Yahlnaaw 2019, 7). As Verwoord, in Verwoord and Smith (2020), asked, "What might it look like to decolonize partnership given that it is a practice and ethos currently situated within a Eurocentric system of education?" (36–37). In summary, although pedagogical partnership may challenge some aspects of dominant academic ontologies, it may fail to fully dismantle and reimagine Eurocentric ontologies that built the academy—perhaps especially as fewer partnerships have thus far specifically and explicitly focused on challenging Eurocentrism.

Going public with partnership work might also create ontological challenges for student partners when academic spaces such as conferences fail to recognize or affirm students' full selves. Additionally, as we wrote in chapter 3, in contrast to dominant ontologies in postsecondary education that are based on one's productivity, labor, or individual contribution, partnership fosters possibilities for personhood that center on mutuality, respect, and recognition. However, in the preparation and dissemination of research conducted in partnership, we may inadvertently be participating in these restrictive ontologies of academia along with their specific forms of communication—and ideas of impact and contribution based on publication records, authorship order, citations, and other metrics that fail to fully recognize our value as people. Other types of partnership work may more easily avoid these restrictive ontologies by focusing on change that is personally observed and felt as meaningful. There is also the potential negative ontological impact of having one's academic work and research rejected during peer review (e.g., disempowerment, misrecognition, never feeling good enough), and contrastingly, the ontological validation (as a scholar, researcher) of being affirmed in this sphere.

Alise describes this challenge more fully, reflecting on their own experiences of participating in partnership and scholarship of teaching and learning (SoTL) conferences:

> I have found it hard to "be" a crazy/disabled/queer person in these spaces in these spaces that have, in my experience, felt very heteronormative and able-bodied, where colleagues don't commonly talk about identifying as Mad or disabled, there isn't much attention to accessibility, people feel highly (heteronormatively) gendered in what they wear and consider "professional" dress and interpersonal etiquette. All of these contextual factors—which can be read as ways of being in partnership spaces and thus ontological—can suppress or fail to affirm difference. I feel concerned for student (and faculty) partners from equity-seeking groups in these spaces. In one presentation I gave about my pedagogical work in Mad(ness) Studies to a SoTL audience (see de Bie 2020 for further context on Mad Studies, associated with the longer history of Critical Disability Studies), I received feedback that I was "cutting edge"—which seemed more about the degree to which my work diverged from the known status quo than a knowledge-

able peer review of its quality. It felt alienating, not affirming. (I don't fit here. People can't understand my work here.) So while partnership spaces may offer different ways of "being" from more hierarchical ontologies, they might simultaneously restrict possibilities for being—such as not presently having the capacity to support me in figuring out Mad, disabled, and queer ways of being a SoTL researcher. (Elizabeth Marquis, Alison Cook-Sather, and Leslie Patricia Luqueño, personal communication, December 2019)

In a number of these examples, the specificity of the students' ethnoracial, disability, queer, and gender identities was significant to their experience, a kind of particularity that is often missed when talking about "students as partners" or student partners from equity-seeking groups as a homogenous population (as often happens in the literature, including this book). A lack of attention to the heterogeneity of students' social locations can negatively affect the possibilities for being recognized and supported through partnership.

## Difficulty of Agency

Students from equity-seeking groups who have lost a sense of self and agency through ontological violence (see chapter 2) may face significant difficulty reclaiming the agency needed to participate in partnership effectively. For example, partnership, despite its collaborative nature, can involve a lot of independent and self-motivated work and rely on student initiative to put forward their ideas. This may be especially difficult for students new to this opportunity, and those who desire a lot of structure, encouragement, and direction. As Marquis, Black, and Healey (2017) have described, some faculty partners have "trouble deciding when to lead and when to fall back to let their partner take on more responsibility" (726; see also Lenihan-Ikin et al. 2020; Mercer-Mapstone, Dvorakova, Groenendijk et al. 2017), a negotiation of power structures that can require a different balance and orientation when working with students desiring structure. In some cases, students may not actually want to participate in a partnership, but may be looking for mentorship or supervision by faculty and staff and their proactive, nonmutual support negotiating postsecondary education.

As Dillon (1997) suggested, even if someone holds an "intellectual understanding" (239) of their self-worth, such as knowing they deserve to be respected as a human being, and gains an accompanying "experiential understanding" (239), perhaps through feeling respected by a faculty or student partner with whom they are collaborating, a person who has been affected by systems of oppression may continue to struggle with fully affirming self-respect. Despite an intellectual and experiential understanding, a person's gut, "primordial interpretation of self and self-worth . . . most profound valuing of [them]selves" (241) may be "incessant[ly] whispering below the

threshold of awareness: 'you're not good enough, you're nothing' . . . [lead-
ing to beliefs that] . . . this is what *I am* most fundamentally, and nothing
I do or become can change that fact" (242). Applied to partnership, there
is certainly literature to support how pedagogical partnerships can facilitate
forms of ontological affirmation and justice—where participating students
feel affirmed in who they are as valued persons. However, Dillon's (1997)
work also acknowledges that while having a new experience of self-respect
as a person and partner can be impactful, it is not always enough to change
someone's deep-seated self-conceptions. The scale, duration, and impact
of institutional violences on students from equity-seeking groups can be
tremendous, and cause significant harms. Partnership on its own may be
insufficient for repairing these ontological injustices, especially when violent
institutional practices persist.

### Recommendations for Mediating Unintentional Contributions to Ontological Harms and Barriers to Justice

To address these potential ontological tensions and limitations, we must
recognize that supporting students from equity-seeking groups in partnership may require, at times, different approaches than typically imagined and
applied in contemporary partnership initiatives. To the extent that it is true
that equity-seeking students have been less likely to apply and participate in
partnership in some cases, then the factors that have led to the past success
of partnership projects may not fully map onto what is needed to support
students from equity-seeking groups in such work. To address the ontological tensions that can be raised by partnership, to avoid contributing unintentionally to harms, and to tackle barriers to facilitating justice through
partnership, we recommend:

- being attentive and responsive to what the terms of partnership signal
  in different contexts and carefully revisiting and potentially revising
  the language used to name partnership work and participants in an
  effort to avoid terms that undermine the espoused premises of the
  work and are potentially damaging to participants, working with the
  fact that no single set of terms will suffice for engaging in and com-
  municating about this work across contexts;
- creating spaces in partnership programs and projects within which
  student partners feel they can bring their whole selves and discuss the
  range of experiences they are having in partnership work, including
  how to balance, reconcile, or manage the tensions and contradictions
  between the selves they feel they need to be for partnership work and
  the selves they need to be for other work and parts of their lives;

- engaging in ongoing, critical reflection about partnership itself and the cultural assumptions and dominant ontologies potentially embedded in it, and revising, responding, or otherwise acting on that reflection as necessary; and
- striving not to homogenize or essentialize student partners who identify as belonging to equity-seeking groups and, instead, exploring, learning from, and creating space for diversity of identity, experience, and perspective of those who are underrepresented in and underserved by postsecondary education and the different kinds of structures and processes they might want or need.

## Conclusion

By viewing tensions through our framework of epistemic, affective, and ontological violences and the harms that result, we raise here a variety of significant complexities, some that are less frequently recognized and discussed in partnership literature. We name them not to dissuade people from engaging in partnership work, but to encourage the pursuit of partnerships in thoughtful and critical ways. When we are aware of these complexities, we are more likely to think differently and expansively about possible challenges, and to take precautions in partnership to mediate possible harm. Although we wholeheartedly support offering partnership opportunities to equity-seeking groups and see the benefit and importance of equitable distribution of opportunity, we are also cautious about the harms that may come to this particular population. Marquis et al. (forthcoming) have pointed out that "there are risks attached to responsibilizing individuals from equity-seeking groups for transforming unjust and oppressive institutions" (see also Mercer-Mapstone, Islam, and Reid 2021). We have discussed many of these risks, including the possibilities of emotional labor and epistemic and ontological remarginalization, throughout this chapter. For partnership to meet its potential to contribute to equity, we need to be attentive to such challenges and find ways to mitigate them.

In addition to the tensions described thus far, we continue to feel uncertain about the degree to which the epistemic, affective, and ontological impacts we have observed may translate beyond those participating in partnership. For example, to what extent do they transfer to students enrolled in courses on which students and faculty collaborate to enhance equity? And in what ways do they affect wider structures on campus? Much of the partnership literature has concentrated its discussion of experiences at the personal level of individual participants, with a focus on students. This book seeks to position these impacts in a broader conceptual framework, though it is primarily focused on violences experienced by and harms done to individual students as members of one or more equity-seeking groups. It explores broader impacts of these themes (e.g., in chapter 3 we consider how affirmation of student knowledge contributes to the production and promotion of different knowledges at a wider scale), challenging us to discern and strive to avoid letting the work partnership does at the individual level reinforce some inequities.

Although some express doubt that partnership might lead to systemic change (see Marquis, Woolmer et al. 2019), the framework we offer in this book may help us begin to address inequities at the structural or institutional level. For instance, one of the reasons we find promise in the principles and practice of partnership, as elaborated in chapter 2, is the greater potential for attending to epistemic, affective, and ontological harms often ignored by more institutional-focused change to structure and policy. By deepening our understanding of these harms through our work in partnership, we are better positioned to extend this analysis to the institutional structures that inflict the epistemic, affective, and ontological violences that cause these harms. As we elaborate in chapter 6, there are examples of how specific partnership projects might sync with broader institutional initiatives beyond the classroom—such as those related to equity, diversity, and inclusion commitments and legislative demands—to effect change at wider scales across postsecondary institutions and have an impact on epistemic, affective, and ontological violences and harms. Likewise, some partnership initiatives have been explicitly and intentionally designed to attempt to foster change at the institutional level (e.g., Cook-Sather et al. 2020; Leota and Sutherland 2020).

Our focus in the preceding pages on the tensions and limitations that may interrupt or mediate the possibility of positive epistemic, affective, and ontological redress at the individual level also fails to fulsomely account for the possible institutional limitations of partnership on equity. For example, the potential for partnership's radical goals to be domesticated or watered down within institutional structures, and for partnership to be taken up and framed in relation to neoliberal discourses (Guitman, Acai, and Mercer-Mapstone 2020; Guitman and Marquis 2020; Matthews, Dwyer et al. 2019; Neary 2016; Neary and Saunders 2016; Woolmer 2018) are real dangers. These considerations merit ongoing attention. Moreover, in a time of social and political tension where violence and injustice at global, state, and institutional scales are having dramatic, urgent, and irreparable effects on the environment and human lives, there is also perhaps some needed caution when choosing to pursue a partnership-based equity intervention that has most of its known impact on individual and interpersonal levels. Partnership may not always be the most appropriate approach in a struggle for greater equity and justice.

# 6

# APPLYING THE FRAMEWORK: INDIVIDUAL REFLECTIONS AND CONTEXTUAL CONSIDERATIONS

In chapter 5 we explored some of the tensions that our conceptual framework surfaces in relation to the pursuit of equity and justice through pedagogical partnership. To balance and move forward from some of the challenges and limitations we identified, we focus in this chapter on further promising directions and possibilities of pedagogical partnership to redress harm and promote epistemic, affective, and ontological justice. Each of us offers an example of how we are integrating, applying, and carrying forward the conceptual framework we have presented here and how it informs practice. We endeavor in these examples to integrate different dimensions of the framework, showing how epistemic, affective, and ontological justice are interwoven in such projects.

Our examples move from individual student experiences (Leslie's and Alise's) as those intersect with institutional and other, larger structures, through raising the possibility of focusing on faculty experience (as one of Beth's current projects, conducted in partnership with other colleagues, does) to describing institution-wide efforts to move toward more equitable and justice-oriented approaches (as some of Alison's recent work endeavors to support). We offer these (imperfect) examples as visions of what is possible so that readers can consider what could be adapted to fit their contexts and to spark and inspire other locally relevant possibilities.

After we share each of these examples, we conclude the chapter by considering how the framework we have offered might be applied, analyzed, and further developed in relation to individuals with different identities and across different contexts. These considerations are intended to support readers in brainstorming visions of the possible for their own contexts.

80

### Linking Students' Knowledge Creation, Passions, and Paid Employment (Leslie)

In 2019 I worked with Dr. Anthony Jack at Harvard University's Graduate School of Education on a sociohistorical analysis of the federal work-study program. This particular example of a research partnership helped me develop communication and pedagogical skills while it also paid me to work in an area that I am interested in pursuing as a career.

Though the work-study program in the United States has been around for approximately 50 years, it has not been widely critiqued or explored by educational scholars (Baum 2019). One of the main issues we found in our research is that there is no federal regulation in the United States on the types of jobs that colleges and universities are able to offer to students who qualify for work-study. Encompassed in the Higher Education Act of 1965, the only guidance higher education institutions receive related to the range of jobs they are able to offer states:

> Jobs located and developed under this section [of the Higher Education Resources and Student Assistance legal code] shall be jobs that are suitable to the scheduling and other needs of [currently enrolled] students and that, to the maximum extent practicable, complement and reinforce the educational or vocational goals of such students. (20 U.S. Code §1087-56)

Because this statute leaves it up to institutions to decide how applicable jobs need to be to vocational and career goals, it means practically any job can be argued to advance these goals "to the maximum extent practicable."

As Jack (2019) demonstrated in his book *The Privileged Poor: How Elite Colleges Are Failing Disadvantaged Students,* the types of work-study jobs available can come at a social cost for students and not advance their educational or career aspirations—a reality that programs like SaLT, Jack contended, work to change:

> Instead of having lower-income undergraduates serve as personal maids for their peers, colleges could provide on-campus jobs that foster skill acquisition, contact with faculty and administrators, and opportunities for enrichment. Bryn Mawr and Haverford Colleges, for example, host the Students as Learners and Teachers (SaLT) program, where students are paid to collaborate with faculty as "pedagogical" partners to enhance innovative teaching at the colleges. (177)

If they are not connected to students' educational or career aspirations, work-study jobs can actually come at a social cost and not only fail to advance educational goals but also be stigmatizing and cause epistemic, affective, and ontological harm. Our work-study project aimed to challenge the permissibility of these jobs and rethink how on-campus employment should help students beyond just a way of making money.

Partnership can be utilized to advance this goal as collaborating with faculty and staff can be an on-campus job that helps students develop communication and pedagogical skills that are beneficial in the long run. Like in the SaLT program, students are paid for their labor, and because many of them are interested in pursuing educational careers, their on-campus job becomes résumé worthy and a platform to build experience before graduation. The SaLT program and similar partnership models, like few other on-campus jobs, provide access to learning about the "behind-the-scenes" aspects of pedagogical planning and classroom organization. SaLT also gives insight into the hidden curriculum—the unintentional lessons taught in postsecondary education that reinforce inequities (Brunson 2018; Cook-Sather et al. 2019). Offering student partnerships as a form of employment has the potential to redefine the work-study program as an approach to viewing on-campus jobs as mutually beneficial for both the student and the employer.

Furthermore, partnership can lead to change in how institutions view on-campus work. In 2019, Haverford College established an institutional Task Force on Work and Service that consisted of faculty, staff, and students who convened to address student employment. Although not explicitly referred to as student partners, the students on the committee worked alongside the other members of the task force to survey approximately 300 students and 85 hiring managers (Elias 2019). By providing expertise about their own experiences with on-campus jobs, the students on the task force provided unique insight that would redefine what work-study looks like at Haverford College. The task force's 2019 report accomplished a wage increase for all student employees and raised consciousness about failures of the college's work-study program, such as the need to prioritize work-study students in on-campus job hiring processes (Elias 2019). Thus, we see how including student partners within larger discussions about work-study and on-campus employment can lead to policy changes informed by people's lived experiences. This is one example of how student partners can contribute to any number of projects within and beyond the classroom to improve student learning experiences in postsecondary education, and potentially the breadth of ways that working in partnership can redress historical epistemic, affective, and ontological injustices on campus.

## Leveraging—or Parting From—Partnerships in Support of Equity Goals (Alise)

Although this book has offered pedagogical partnership as one strategy for advancing equity beyond the narrow requirements of human rights legislation, we can also work in partnership to support such legislation (e.g., employment equity, accessibility). It is thus worthwhile exploring alignment between equity-focused partnerships and other equity initiatives on campus. For example, McMaster University has developed an Equity, Diversity, and Inclusion (EDI) Strategy that names teaching/learning within one of four pillars (McMaster University 2019), and pedagogical partnerships have an important role to play in this area. Our campus has also been facilitating a variety of employment equity initiatives that target permanent and continuing employees, but also contract and short-term staff, including student staff. Some of the equity initiatives underway in our Student Partners Program have been subsidized by institutional funding provided to campus employers to support recruitment of students from equity-seeking groups. Additionally, several partnership projects have taken place in collaboration with our campus Equity and Inclusion Office, Accessibility Council, and Student Accommodation Office, and in the pursuit of compliance with accessibility-related legislative requirements (Brown et al. 2020; de Bie and Brown 2017; Sayles with de Bie 2018). Other partnership projects have supported the institution's commitments to community engagement (Office of Community Engagement 2018) and are exploring the creation of educational resources in support of the Truth and Reconciliation Commission of Canada's (2012) Calls to Action. Partnership between students and faculty, but also between our teaching and learning center and other campus units with some responsibility for equity and inclusion, is thus an important area for further conversation.

We have argued in this book for the possibilities of partnership, but there may be times when a partnership approach between students and staff and faculty is not always what is needed. Several complicated examples come to mind. For example, I was a student partner on a project where my staff partner left their position and I, along with another student partner, became hired as the "staff" coleads. This change in role granted us considerably more freedom to design the initiative than we had in a student–staff partnership where the more institutionally linked staff person was ultimately the lead and responsible for the end deliverables. I also collaborated as a graduate student with a group of undergraduates on a pedagogical project to facilitate change in our School of Social Work. We "partnered" with a faculty member as far as to have their name as a sponsor of our application to meet eligibility criteria for "student partnership" funding (which required listing a staff or faculty member as a partner), but felt it more appropriate to partner between students than with faculty directly (de Bie et al. 2017). Most recently I have been supporting a student funded through our Student Partners Program on a project that began as a paper they wrote for a course that I taught. Rather than contribute as an "equal" partner where we share responsibility for collaborative work, my role has tended more toward that of a cheerleader and institutional navigator as the student claimed ownership of the project, collecting and analyzing data. In this case, "partnership" from me in the form of more active involvement could be a kind of theft, appropriation, patronization, or interference.

Aside from more narrowly understood conceptions of partnerships, then, between students and staff or faculty, I'm also invested in supporting (and finding money to fund) student–student partnerships, or initiatives designed and pursued by students (Rhoads, Buenavista, and Maldonado 2004). For me, it is not just that partnership can cause harm or fail to facilitate justice and redress—but that it may not always be the needed or best approach, and it certainly isn't the only one. There are times when separatism or refusal has an important role to play (student-only and student-led projects, ditching one's faculty or staff colleague, pulling out of a project that doesn't align with our values and goals, grassroots and noninstitutionalized approaches). For example, there may be times when:

- it is more epistemically validating to engage in student initiatives and share and develop knowledge among students without staff than it is to collaborate;
- student-led initiatives are freer to communicate more radical ideas and thus affirm rather than censor student knowledge (Maldonado, Rhoads, and Buenavista 2005);
- student initiatives require less emotional labor than working in partnership with employees of the institution (where there may be more concern with staff feelings or perspectives);
- taking action without staff or faculty contributes in important and different ways to reducing alienation, building social networks, and enhancing self-empowerment (Maldonado, Rhoads, and Buenavista 2005); and
- there is more ontological benefit for students to be affirmed as separatist activists than there is in being a student "partner."

This is especially imperative if our ultimate desire is equity and justice, which, at times, may not be achieved through partnership. Despite definitions that suggest partnership is "a collaborative, reciprocal process through which all participants have the opportunity to contribute equally, although not necessarily in the same ways, to curricular or pedagogical conceptualization, decision-making, implementation, investigation, or analysis" (Cook-Sather, Bovill, and Felten 2014, 6–7), when equity and justice are the goal, reciprocity and equal contribution may not be.

Faculty can work with students in a range of ways besides partnership to advance social justice (creating coalitions, mentoring in activism strategies, gathering financial resources) (Kezar, Bertram Gallant, and Lester 2011). Furthermore, staff and faculty practitioners of partnership who recognize the legitimacy of student knowledge may be able to ease contentious relationships between student activists and university staff and administration. Instead of student activists experiencing these staff as gatekeepers, antagonists, or enemies, and staff perceiving these students as a disruptive nuisance (Anderson 2019; Hoffman and Mitchell 2016; Ropers-Huilman, Carwile, and Barnett 2005), working in partnership can increase our appreciation of student activism and the support we offer student-led struggle for greater equity on campus.

Consequently, my hopes for partnership are for us to more fully consider how to support student activists and initiatives, explore circumstances in which partnership may be more likely to cause harm or another approach may be more likely to provide redress, and create space for conversation about the complexities of partnership such that the possibilities of *not* partnering are also maintained. The framework developed throughout this book can apply to other types of equity initiatives (like student-led ones) by facilitating greater recognition of the harms a specific approach to advancing equity might be well suited to address, as well as examination of the factors that may limit or get in the way of an approach's potential contribution to justice. I hope this opens up different ways of thinking and acting as we use a variety of strategies to challenge persistent inequities on campus and beyond.

## Applying Our Framework to Considerations of Equity Affecting Faculty and Staff (Beth)

Although there are many examples of research and reflective writing exploring faculty experiences of partnership (e.g., Cook-Sather 2014, 2015, 2020; Cook-Sather and Abbot 2016; Cook-Sather, Bahti, and Ntem 2019; Cook-Sather and Des-Ogugua 2019; Cook-Sather and Felten 2017b; Cook-Sather, Gauthier, and Foster 2020; Cook-Sather et al. 2017; Kupatadze 2019; Marquis 2018; Marquis, Power, and Yin 2019), some have noted that the research literature has focused extensively on *student* outcomes and experiences (Kandiko Howson and Weller 2016; Mercer-Mapstone, Dvorakova, Matthews et al. 2017). Although we likewise attend in this book to the ways in which partnership might contribute to redressing some of the epistemic, affective, and ontological harms experienced by students who identify as members of equity-seeking groups, it remains the case that faculty and staff who claim membership in such groups likewise experience significant forms of marginalization and injustice in postsecondary institutions (Daniel 2019; James 2012; Joseph and Hirshfield 2011; Martinez, Chang, and Welton 2017; Pittman 2010; Waterfield, Beagan, and Weinberg 2018). As someone who occupies various locations of social and institutional privilege and who has advocated and facilitated pedagogical partnership—particularly highlighting its potential to contribute to more equitable and just institutions—I've become increasingly conscious of the extent to which it is incumbent on me to attend more fully to such faculty and staff experiences when considering partnership's potential contributions to equity. To this end, I've recently been working with several colleagues on a research project that seeks to explore faculty and staff experiences and perceptions of partnership in relation to their intersecting social locations and institutional positions (Marquis, Guitman et al. 2020; Marquis, Woolmer et al. 2019). We aimed, in this work, to understand how faculty and staff (from institutions in four countries) understand partnership and its potential relationships to equity, given the differing ways in which their social locations affect their experiences in the academy.

One of the most notable findings coming out of this early research was just how widely participants' perspectives and experiences varied (Marquis, Guitman et al. 2020; Marquis, Woolmer et al. 2019). Although many suggested that their identities had little influence on their experiences of the academy or of partnership, others shared experiences that affirmed and echoed the literature documenting the harms and injustices experienced by equity-seeking faculty in postsecondary education institutions, and pointed toward ways in which these experiences can encourage, discourage, or otherwise affect working in partnership. Some equity-seeking faculty and staff suggested that partnership presented a valued opportunity to work in solidarity with similarly located students, for instance, or pointed out that their own experiences of marginalization made them powerfully aware of the need to work in partnership to counter institutional inequities. At the same time, some also made comments suggesting that the challenges they experienced as marginalized faculty—including increased demands on their time and challenges to their knowledge and expertise—could make partnership feel difficult or risky. Whereas some partnership work has tended to focus on power differentials between faculty and students, sometimes implicitly overlooking distinctions within those groups, our findings suggest we need to attend more fully to how power operates *within* faculty and student populations, and to continue to develop more complex theorizations of power in partnership that take into account more than the authority accorded to faculty by virtue of their institutional roles (see also Matthews 2017; Matthews, Cook-Sather et al. 2019; Mercer-Mapstone, Islam, and Reid 2021; Verwoord and Smith 2020).

This project, as well as other work beginning to foreground the voices of marginalized faculty and staff participating in partnership (e.g., Cook-Sather 2020; Cook-Sather and Agu, 2013; Kupatadze 2019; Perez 2016), has been foremost in my mind as we developed and worked through the framework presented in this book. Although our attention has necessarily been focused on student experiences, I'm curious to think further about if and how the conceptualization of epistemic, affective, and ontological harms we have articulated here might (or might not) apply to faculty and staff experiences, and about the extent to which partnership might (or might not) contribute to redressing and/or reproducing those harms. Indeed, I hope that the framework we present in this book offers tools that can be applied to considerations of institutional equity more broadly, and thus help refine partnership's capacity to contribute to equity both for students and for faculty and staff going forward.

## Creating Institutional Structures That Sustain Equity Work (Alison)

When, in 2007, I supported five faculty and five students of color in piloting Bryn Mawr and Haverford College's SaLT program, there was no campus-wide discourse about diversity, equity, and inclusion, as there is now. We now have at both Bryn Mawr and Haverford Colleges frameworks, websites, and numerous other initiatives focused specifically on diversity, equity, and inclusion, and, more recently, antiracist work. Both separate from and, increasingly, in partnership with others in these institutions, I have maintained SaLT's goal of making classrooms more equitable and inclusive. It has been striking and (tentatively) hopeful to see how that originally liminal pilot has evolved into an institutional structure—working in pedagogical partnership with a student is now an option offered to all incoming faculty as part of a pedagogy seminar (most new faculty have chosen to participate) and to all faculty as a stand-alone option (over half the faculty have participated) (Cook-Sather 2016)—consistent with larger institutional commitments at both colleges to diversity, equity, and inclusion. Enhancing educational equity is also, increasingly, the goal of individual, stand-alone partnerships between faculty and SaLT student consultants and, in response to the intersection of the global pandemic and the uprisings as part of the Black Lives Matter movement in the summer of 2020, the explicit focus of partnership work became how to take a trauma-informed, antiracist approach to course planning for the 2020–2021 academic year.

Other recent work promises to even more substantially and explicitly foreground pedagogical partnership as a means to redress the harms marginalized students have experienced as a result of the violence of postsecondary education. In the spring 2019 semester, supported by a grant awarded to Haverford College from the Lumina Foundation and drawing as well on resources from the SaLT program and the Haverford College Provost's Office, I facilitated a seminar called "Toward Greater Equity, Inclusion, and Belonging Within and Beyond Our Classrooms." Ten faculty members who claimed different identities—including many that are underrepresented in higher education—participated in weekly 2-hour meetings in which they explored equity-focused practices they already use and approaches they had not yet considered or tried. Each faculty participant also worked in a one-on-one partnership with a student consultant through the SaLT program to analyze what was already happening to foster equity and inclusion in classrooms, departments, and centers on campus and to gather a wide range of student perspectives to inform efforts to further equity and inclusion both in the individual faculty members' classrooms and at departmental, divisional, and institutional levels.

In the context of that seminar, some faculty and student partners focused on course-level changes that would affect not only the focal course but also subsequent courses. For instance, Benjamin Le worked with his student partner, Maya Gorstein, who described themselves as in the "multiracial, sexual and gender minority" (Le and Gorstein, 2019, p. 2), to change the dynamics around class discussion such that a greater diversity of students could speak and have their contributions valued, thereby pursuing epistemic justice. Brook Lillehaughen worked with her student partner, Elisa Cooney, to restructure homework, which, as Lillehaugen explained, "tends to unequally impact students that already have numerous external pressures on their time and energy including work schedules, health concerns, and family obligations" (Lillehaugen and Cooney, 2019, 2). Alleviating some of the affective harm inflicted by this institutional practice, the changes "took pressure off" and "helped me stress less" (Lillehaugen and Cooney 2019, 3), according to students surveyed about the change.

Faculty and student partners also conducted focus groups with students and developed approaches to making departmental practices more welcoming to a diversity of students. For instance, Kathryne Corbin revised her practice in all classes based on her student partner, Carol Lee Diallo's, advice (Corbin and Diallo 2019):

Even though French is a gendered language, there are ways to speak to people without gendering them. Using their name instead of a pronoun, for example, or even making students aware that gender-neutral pronouns and inclusive language are emerging in French, too. Knowing about more inclusive pronouns is important so students who don't identify with gendered pronouns can still fully participate and engage in class—and feel respected and recognized! (2)

Also working at the departmental level, student partner Amaka Eze and faculty partner Ken Koltun-Fromm worked together to learn from students how they experienced the Religion Department curriculum at Haverford College. Taking on established (and sometimes entrenched) institutional structures is difficult work that requires and activates vulnerabilities. Eze explained that "learning to trust in one another's expertise and commitment" necessitated "transparency and vulnerability," and she suggested that, "by leaning in to the discomfort of our relationship, and of our very different positionalities, Ken and I were able to better identify systemic issues within the department and propose new channels for authentic collaboration" (Koltun-Fromm and Eze 2019, 2).

The interpersonal, emotional, as well as intellectual dimensions of partnership are what can reiterate or redress the harms we name in our conceptual framework, and supporting Eze and Koltun-Fromm as they worked through their discomfort was a very concrete way in which I sought to put that framework into practice. Another faculty–student partnership that same semester focused on making student experiences in the natural sciences division "an intentional, equitable environment for all" (Wynkoop quoted in White and Wynkoop 2019, 2)—work endeavored through "conversations [that] created a space of care, kindness, and patience—all qualities necessary to do work that at times can seem overwhelming and insurmountable" (2). The revisions at the classroom, departmental, and divisional levels were informed not only by the student partners with whom these faculty worked but also by a range of students from equity-seeking groups whose contributions affirmed their knowledge, lived experiences, and being at the institution—steps toward epistemic, affective, and ontological justice.

During the fall 2019 semester, these same five faculty and five new Haverford College colleagues elected to participate in another seminar, this one called "Navigating/Transforming." This seminar was supported by the Hurford Center for Arts and Humanities, the Provost's Office, the Center for Peace and Global Citizenship, and the Koshland Integrated Natural Sciences Center at Haverford. This cross-center funding signaled a new level of institutional support for the work of the seminar, which was developing a multiyear, cocreated, cocurricular course that would offer a multiyear, single teaching credit to faculty members and one-quarter course credit per semester for students. The multiyear, cocurricular, collaboratively created course aims to provide students opportunities to: develop the cultural capital and the language to successfully navigate the institution as it is; affirm and deploy their lived experiences, knowledge, skills, and cultural backgrounds to challenge normative institutional culture and help create a departmental and institutional culture more welcoming and equitable to a diversity of students; and contribute to an evolving curriculum for future students. The course aims to provide faculty opportunities to be recognized and compensated for the time they spend on mentoring and advising, develop insights into what students bring and can contribute to not only this curriculum but also a cultural shift in the department and at the college overall, and support students and faculty in partnering to foster a sense of belonging *and* transform institutional culture (Cook-Sather and Lillehaugen 2020; Cook-Sather et al. 2020). My work to support this continuation of the previous semester's conversation and move to sustain spaces for such conversation feels like the most concrete example in my 25 years at Bryn Mawr and Haverford Colleges of how this work might be institutionalized. The course, called Belonging and Becoming at Haverford College, was approved in the spring 2020 semester for the 2020–2021 academic year.

The institutional structure for navigating and transforming institutional structures and practices that we have created at Haverford College in the form of this course was inspired by approaches developed at Trinity Washington University and Radford University, both of which have received Howard Hughes Medical Institute Inclusive Excellence grants (Sible et al. 2019). It is also guided by the promise of pedagogical partnership to redress epistemic, affective, and ontological harms through developing not only attitudes and practices but also structures that support greater equity and justice. Faculty and students will work together over multiple years in a cocurricular structure to name and change inequitable institutional structures and practices. They will engage in what Shittu (2020), who enrolled in the course, described as necessary, "honest and painful discussion, where the voices of those most marginalized are elevated—and put into action" (para. 11).

As someone with many privileged dimensions of sociocultural identity, a stable institutional position, and a strong voice in international conversations about pedagogical partnership, I have not in the past and do not now experience many of the forms of epistemic, affective, and ontological violence we discuss or the harms that result. But because of my role as director of a partnership program and my political, personal, and pedagogical commitments, I have a responsibility—consistent with my commitments and my desire—to use the forms of power and access I have to promote equity, in part through listening to, learning from, and being guided by those who do experience the forms of violence and harm we discuss. I am hopeful that the institutional support reflected in the funding provided for these two recent seminars and the new course is indicative of an institutional-level commitment to furthering equity and justice.

## Considering the Framework's Applicability to Diverse Individual, Institutional, and National Contexts

To conclude this chapter, we highlight other ways these goals could be pursued, specifically in relation to exploring how the framework might apply (and be adapted and revised) across wide-ranging individual experiences of partnership and diverse institutional and national contexts.

Although many of the students who have worked in pedagogical partnership through our programs claim one or more of the equity-seeking identities we name in chapter 1, we neither assume nor mean to imply that the experiences of students within or across these groups are uniform, or that students with these—and other—identities would have the same experiences in different contexts. Complex intersections of identity within and between partners lead to equally complex ways in which partnership can both redress and exacerbate epistemic, affective, and ontological harms. Therefore, one of our hopes is that others will take the conceptual framework we have offered and use it to try to better understand the experiences of individual students given the particular, intersecting dimensions of identity they experience and how those play out in their particular postsecondary educational contexts.

One challenge of accessing and analyzing different students' experiences is how, on the one hand, to illuminate particular kinds of experience and, on the other, to maintain anonymity and confidentiality, so as not to make students more vulnerable or inflict further violence or harm. Perhaps striving to achieve this balance, much partnership scholarship does not provide demographic information on student participants, and it is typically reflective essays or other more personal reports that parse out individuals' unique experiences. As conveyed in chapter 3, much partnership literature has focused on role (student) and on racialized dimensions of identity (e.g., Cook-Sather and Agu 2013; Cook-Sather and Des-Ogugua 2019; Cook-Sather and Seay, 2020) and gender (Cates, Madigan, and Reitenauer 2018; Mercer-Mapstone, Guitman, and Acai 2019). There is also a growing set of arguments about international students' experiences (Colón García 2017; Stanway et al. 2019), and Alise has been working on several disability-specific projects (Brown et al. 2020; de Bie 2020; de Bie and Raaper 2019). We hope that the framework we provide, as well as the discussion of how we apply it to our own work and what we see as limitations and other possibilities, will be helpful to others who are positioned to explore particular dimensions and intersections of individual students', and faculty and staff members', identities.

Although we are writing from two specific locations in North America—the United States and Canada—and, further, from particular institutional locations within that part of the world, we recognize that there are differences between contexts that affect how dimensions of identity are perceived, defined, and responded to. Healey and Healey (2018) have noted that much depends on context in regard to how partnership work might be developed, a point corroborated by scholarship that explicitly considers the specificities of working in or toward partnership in particular national, cultural, or institutional milieux (e.g., Chng 2019; Kaur and Yong Bing 2020; Seow 2019; Sim 2019; Waqar and Asad 2020). We hope that others will use the framework we offer to analyze national and institutional contexts and the scholarship on partnership produced in those contexts to surface the particular forms of violence and harm underrepresented students have experienced.

We have applied the framework, retrospectively, to our own programs, and we hope to learn whether further insights would emerge if other programs and individual initiatives were analyzed through the terms of the framework. We would be equally interested in how pedagogical partnership initiatives that launched with an explicit commitment to equity and inclusion and those that did not might make use of and extend the framework. We note here a few examples of classroom- and curriculum-focused pedagogical partnership programs within the United States based on the SaLT model that articulated an explicit commitment, two programs outside the U.S. context that explicitly embraced an equity focus, and several that found that equity emerged even though they were not the initial focus of the partnership work. We mention those here both to acknowledge their work and to pose questions regarding the use and extension of our framework in their diverse contexts.

Within the United States, Smith College, a selective liberal arts college for women in the northeastern region of the United States, claimed as the founding goal for its partnership program developing a more inclusive learning environment through engaging in pedagogical partnerships around "bias interrupters and inclusive curricular development" (Cook-Sather, Bahti, and Ntem 2019, p. 227). Berea College, a small, private liberal arts college in east central Kentucky that serves promising students who come from limited economic means—97% of students are eligible for government grants, based on family income; all receive complete tuition scholarships worth about $100,000 over 4 years—developed a pedagogical partnership program as part of a grant focused on "Belonging, Inclusive Excellence, and Student Learning" (Cook-Sather, Ortquist-Ahrens, and Reynolds 2019). And finally, Florida Gulf Coast University, a midsized, master's-level member of the State University System of Florida, developed a pedagogical partnership program as part of a wider university student success initiative and at the intersection of faculty development and student success (Cook-Sather, Bahti, and Ntem 2019; Cook-Sather, Ortquist-Ahrens, and Reynolds 2019; Gennocro and Straussberger 2020). Would students' experiences in programs such as these be similar to or different from the experiences we have referenced throughout the book when analyzed through the conceptual framework we provide? Likewise, how might insights from these programs inflect and modify the framework and the possibilities and tensions attached to it that we discuss here?

Two pedagogical partnership programs outside the United States explicitly committed to equity have been influenced by the SaLT model as well as developed in response to their own particular contexts and institutional commitments. For instance, Ako in Action at the research-intensive Victoria University of Wellington in Aotearoa/New Zealand is a partnership program cocreated by students and academic staff linked to the university's bicultural approach to teaching and learning and built on the Māori term *Ako*, which means both to teach and to learn (Lenihan-Ikin et al. 2020; Leota and Sutherland 2020). And at Kaye Academic College of Education in Beer-Sheva, Israel, which prepares preservice teachers for all compulsory school subjects, student–faculty pairs work in classroom-focused partnerships that are part of the larger institutional commitment to equity and justice for the Jewish and Bedouin populations in the region (Cook-Sather, Bahti, and Ntem 2019; Narkiss and Naaman 2020). What might the framework developed in this book contribute to the partnership work being done in these contexts, and how might scholars in these contexts adapt, amend, or enhance the framework or replace it with something more locally applicable?

Looking beyond these specific examples, one might note that individual and institutional partnership initiatives have been developed in a growing range of countries around the world, including China (Huijser et al. 2019), Hong Kong (Chen and Ho 2020; Ho 2017; Pounder, Ho Hung-lam, and Groves 2016), the Netherlands (Van Dam 2016), Norway (Wallin and Aarsand 2019), Pakistan (Waqar and Asad 2020), Singapore (Chng 2019), and Sweden (Barrineau and Anderson 2018; Bergmark and Westman 2016), to name just a few. One example can be found at Universiti Utara Malaysia, a large public university in the north of Malaysia, where Amrita Kaur and Toh Yong Bing worked in partnership on one of Kaur's courses. Reflecting on this partnership, Kaur explained that her student partner, Toh Yong Bing, who is "from a minority community in Malaysia," was "able to draw my attention to the importance of highlighting the social differences in Malaysian society and ways to handle those differences through educational initiatives" (Kaur and Yong Bing 2020, 67). What might we learn about epistemic, affective, and ontological harm in this context, and about forms of repair and justice? In what ways, if any, might the framework we have developed in our North American institutional contexts be useful in an Asian context? As further research is published in additional contexts on equity and on partnership, the theories and evidence offered by these local examples may not fit within the wider framework that was built around the existing partnership literature. What modifications or alternative frameworks might be necessary to better explore partnership and equity in Malaysian postsecondary institutions, and in other contexts around the world? Even if the original focus of pedagogical partnership work might not be explicitly on equity, such a focus can emerge and might be supported by our framework and extended as the framework is revised.

In chapter 1 we articulated that our goals in writing this book were to encourage and contribute to the development of theories of pedagogical partnership in general and in relation to equity-focused impacts, and to affirm the urgency of work that opens up alternate ways of thinking, feeling, being, relating, and moving to advance justice. The examples and hopes we offer from our respective perspectives in this chapter point to some ways that our work has contributed and may further contribute to realizing these goals. We have also introduced some collective ruminations on how the conceptual framework developed in this book might apply and be adapted and revised to further recognize partnership's capacity to redress harm and facilitate justice across the diverse individual, institutional, and national contexts in which it is practiced.

# 7

# RECOMMENDATIONS AND REMAINING QUESTIONS

In this final chapter of the book, we look back over the work of the previous chapters and conclude with some recommendations and remaining questions.

We opened this book with an assertion in chapter 1 that students, staff, and faculty members from equity-seeking groups have experienced the university as an exclusive institution, and that such exclusion constitutes violence and causes multiple forms of harm. Evoking some of the terms that have been employed in institutional efforts to address a lack of diversity, equity, and inclusion, we noted the way in which many of these have proved inadequate—both the actions and the terms that can serve more as appeasement than contributions to action, redress of harm, or transformation. We offered pedagogical partnership as one, although certainly not the only, approach to illuminating a lack of attention to the harms that marginalized students experience in postsecondary educational institutions.

The conceptual framework we offered in chapter 2, grounded in the lived experiences of students from equity-seeking groups in postsecondary education and in various bodies of scholarship, unpacked a series of epistemic, affective, and ontological violences and resulting harms that these students face. As the way a problem is framed both enables certain solutions and eclipses others (Iverson 2007), we focused on these more specific and precise ways of describing violences and associated harms so that particular nuances and dimensions of these students' struggles would become more perceptible.

In chapter 3 we applied the conceptual framework to the pedagogical partnership literature, which allowed us to highlight how partnership scholarship has offered examples of efforts to redress epistemic, affective, and ontological harms without typically using that language. By rereading the literature in the terms offered by our conceptual framework, we began to illuminate how partnership can meaningfully and intentionally contribute to redressing epistemic, affective, and ontological harm to bring about greater justice. As in chapter 2, drawing on students' own ways of naming their experiences to substantiate our claims is another way in which we endeavor to redress the harms so many of these students experience.

Grounding our conceptual framework in case studies of our two programs in chapter 4 afforded us an opportunity to reread our partnership work in a way that parallels our rereading of partnership literature, and to more fully recognize how our partnership practice may facilitate epistemic, affective, and ontological effects. Doing so also models two potential applications of our framework.

The literature- and practice-based analyses in chapters 3 and 4, respectively, throw into relief some of the complexities our framework surfaces, including the conditions under which partnerships themselves may risk reproducing epistemic, affective, or ontological harms, or prevent the realization of intended and possible epistemic, affective, and ontological redress. In chapter 5 we explored these complexities, reconsidering tensions already well recognized in the partnership literature and bringing to light other, less known and discussed challenges that require our attention if partnership is to contribute to greater justice.

In chapter 6 we drew on each of our own experiences to offer reflections on promising directions for and possibilities of pedagogical partnership to redress harm and promote epistemic, affective, and ontological justice. We also shared considerations regarding how the framework introduced in this book might be used and further developed across diverse sites of partnership practice.

This final chapter summarizes several overarching themes developed through the book, framed as questions we argue need to be asked perpetually:

- What would it look like to consider equity and justice throughout all aspects of partnership?
- How might we invite critique, consider possible harms, and enable ongoing reflection during partnership work?
- What are some ways of sustaining ourselves in the challenging work of promoting equity and justice through partnership?

We address each of these in the following section, followed by a section that reframes and supplements existing recommendations from the partnership literature by considering these in relation to our framework and the process of redressing harm and injustice and contributing to equity through partnership specifically. As such, we conclude with encouragement and a set of recommendations, aspirations, and invitations to join us in ongoing examination of the intersections among partnership, equity, and justice.

## What Would It Look Like to Consider Equity and Justice Throughout All Aspects of Partnership?

We recommend considering what equity and justice in pedagogical partnership means and can look like at all stages, from conceptualizing through launching, developing, sustaining, and disseminating ideas from partnership initiatives. When launching partnership programs or projects, consider who is present, in which kinds of roles, and how equity might be embedded from the outset. Programs such as SaLT (at Bryn Mawr and Haverford Colleges) and Ako in Action (at Victoria University of Wellington in New Zealand), for instance, were conceptualized and launched through partnerships with students and focused on culturally responsive practices from the outset (see Cook-Sather 2018a, 2019; Lenihan-Ikin et al. 2020; Leota and Sutherland 2020). Such practices focus on creating what Tatum (2015) has called the ABCs of "climates of engagement" in which students can succeed. *A* stands for affirming identity, *B* stands for building community, and *C* stands for cultivating leadership.

When recruiting and hiring student partners, it is essential to consider who feels invited and able to participate, and to implement proactive strategies for enhancing equity in recruitment (e.g., focused advertising, in-person question sessions, using ambassadors to support outreach and recruitment, anonymous review of applications, recording and tracking of applicants' demographic data) (Bindra et al. 2018; Bovill et al. 2016; de Bie 2020; Marquis et al. 2018; Mercer-Mapstone, Islam, and Reid 2021). A growing body of partnership scholarship focused on questions of equity and inclusion has taken up this issue of access to partnership opportunities (e.g., Bindra et al. 2018; Bovill et al. 2016; Felten et al. 2013; Marquis, Jayaratnam et al. 2019; Mercer-Mapstone and Bovill 2020; Mercer-Mapstone, Islam, and Reid 2021; Moore-Cherry et al. 2016; O'Shea 2018). Although we agree that such concerns are central, the conceptual framework we present in chapter 2 and use to revisit partnership literature in chapter 3 also asks us to think about partnership's response to (in)equity and injustice in more expansive terms. Partnership's potential relationship to equity, this framework suggests, is more than an issue of distribution (which students are afforded the opportunity to *do* partnership); it is also an issue of recognition and redress of a range of epistemic, affective, and ontological harms and, thereby, a contribution to the pursuit of justice at these levels. Importantly, this does not discount the significance of access and distribution. On the contrary, access to partnership opportunities might be seen as *particularly* important if partnership provides a form of redress for the overlapping forms of injustice and violence in the academy that our framework identifies.

Within partnerships, we must ensure that every participant is valued for what they bring and that partners receive the support they need to engage as fully as they can and wish to. Rather than focus on everyone giving and getting the same thing, a common misperception about partnership (Cook-Sather, Bahti, and Ntem 2019; Cook-Sather, Bovill, and Felten 2014), we recommend attending carefully to the *differences* in what partners bring, contribute, need. This might look like resisting the inclination to default to a generic and homogenous notion of "student" as partner, instead considering the multiple locations that partners occupy (de Bie 2020). It might also look like supporting students as they and their faculty partners identify particular areas of experience and expertise that students bring and, as Leslie pointed out in her discussion in chapter 6 of linking students' knowledge creation, passions, and paid employment, finding ways to support equity work students are already doing or that particularly matters to them. Flexibility is essential to enhancing inclusion in partnership work—such as flexibility in timelines, deadlines, project length, milestones, and partnership modes (Brown et al. 2020; Mercer-Mapstone, Islam, and Reid 2021). This is perhaps especially crucial for including students with disabilities, who may need access to entitled workplace accommodations and may not be familiar with negotiating these in an employment context on campus. As discussed in chapter 5, we also need to attend to the ways in which partnership itself might cause harm to members of equity-seeking groups, and to proactively attempt to prevent and mitigate such harms. We return to this issue in the discussion of our next question.

Additionally, we recommend ongoing rethinking of the language we use in equity-seeking work and the practices that come to reflect our conceptual understandings. In writing this book, we noted terms, such as *diversity, equity, inclusion,* that have shaped people's understandings and experiences of both equity-focused work and partnership work. The meanings of and associations with these terms have shifted and will continue to shift over time, and so they need to be revisited and revised as part of the ongoing process of clarifying the intersections of justice work and partnership work. Although we started out conceptualizing and writing about this work in terms of exclusion, inclusion, and in/equity, we shifted to the language of epistemic, affective, and ontological harm, redress, and justice because the former did not seem strong or precise enough to capture either the lived experiences of students, as Alexis Giron notes in her Foreword, or the kind of change we were striving to name and effect. Developing alternative interpretive resources has enabled us to understand and engage in partnership in new and different ways. A related question of language is how partnership work itself is named. We invite consideration of which language will best contribute to furthering justice in particular, local contexts.

It is also worth considering further if and how partnership projects might contribute to equity and justice when they are not explicitly or specifically focused on equity or justice goals. Although we have argued here for the importance of naming inequity and violence in overt and concrete terms, and of prioritizing action that identifies and redresses associated harms, it is also true that projects that may not be specifically designed to address inequity and injustice can facilitate positive personal experiences for student partners from equity-seeking groups and that involving these students can draw attention to equity issues that may not otherwise have been prioritized. Cook-Sather, Bahti, and Ntem (2019) also pointed out that explicitly naming a focus on equity might lead to quicker rejection or resistance from some faculty (see also Jones-Devitt et al. 2017). In turn, such resistance to equity could expose students working in equity-focused partnerships to a greater likelihood of harm and further injustice. The question of when and how to name a focus on equity and justice thus merits ongoing consideration.

In moving forward, any existing partnership program or project could begin to consider how it might address equity and justice, whether or not this had been made explicit in the program's or project's design. After developing a general program, McMaster University has since piloted a specific equity stream, but there are also ways of embedding considerations of equity in mainstream programs without a complete overhaul of the structure. Keep in mind, too, starting small is still a start! Individual partnership efforts that unfold outside of any programmatic structures, such as those described by Kaur and Yong Bing (2020), make a difference. And finally, people may over time consider more structural shifts to advance equity and justice in their programming or in their individual efforts (e.g., paying attention to equity in recruitment, providing equity-focused training and workshops for partnership participants, articulating equity as a priority focus for partnerships), or they might see, as Alison did in her work, a shift in institutional priorities that allows what might start as an implicit and not-always-articulated-out-loud commitment to become an explicit and named one (Cook-Sather, Bahti, and Ntem 2019; Cook-Sather and Bala 2020).

In light of the critique raised by Patton et al. (2019) that institutions often "add" equity and diversity initiatives, programs, and services without addressing the root causes of oppression and injustice, it is vital that whatever work we do in partnership to advance equity and justice, we really are targeting root causes of violence and harm, rather than "adding in" engagement opportunities without making substantive, structural change to historically elite and exclusionary institutions.

## How Might We Invite Critique, Consider Possible Harms, and Enable Ongoing Reflection During Partnership Work?

Some partnership literature has been faulted for perhaps focusing primarily on positive outcomes and experiences of partnership (Mercer-Mapstone, Dvorakova, Groenendijk et al. 2017; Mercer-Mapstone, Dvorakova, Matthews et al. 2017), in spite of acknowledging challenges attached to factors like navigating power differentials and facing resistance (Bovill et al. 2016; Kehler, Verwoord, and Smith 2017; Marquis, Black, and Healey 2017). At the same time, some recent scholarship has begun to point toward important critiques of partnership, particularly as it relates to equity and justice (de Bie 2020; de Bie and Raaper 2019; Yahlnaaw 2019). Rather than positioning such critique as undesirable or responding to it defensively, we argue that open and ongoing critical analysis is vital to enhancing partnership's capacity to contribute to more equitable and just institutions (see also Guitman, Acai, and Mercer-Mapstone 2020). Given the resilience of power imbalances and the difficulty of dismantling oppressive systems and structures, it seems inevitable that partnership efforts will sometimes falter or fall short of their aims; this should be acknowledged, not as a means of excusing potential problems, but as a starting point for meaningful reflection, discussion, and, where necessary, change (Marquis 2019). In particular, we encourage those interested in partnership as a potential strategy for working toward more equitable and just institutions to actively invite and attempt to respond meaningfully to concerns about partnership—particularly from those who identify as members of equity-seeking groups. Doing so is yet another way to facilitate epistemic justice through the affirmation of those raising these critiques as offering valuable and legitimate knowledge to the conversation. Gibson (2015) has noted that "genuine forms of inclusive provision must start from [a] political premise, acknowledging that there is and needs to be conflict" (884).

Throughout this book, we have considered extensively the ways in which participating in pedagogical partnership might contribute to the redress of epistemic, affective, and ontological harms experienced by students belonging to equity-seeking groups. Nevertheless, we have also pointed to potential risks and challenges for marginalized students who participate in partnership, including the possibility of further harm in some cases and contexts.

This tension underscores the need to proactively consider ways to mitigate the potential harms of partnership and support students navigating the process of partnering with faculty or staff. The possibility that partnership might become akin to a form of cultural taxation (Joseph and Hirshfield 2011), or inappropriately responsibilize people from equity-seeking groups for transforming oppressive systems or educating others about inequity (Mercer-Mapstone, Islam, and Reid 2021), also demands careful attention.

In order to better understand the possibilities of partnership in terms of advancing equity and justice, we need to explore and develop new theorizations, adapt and disrupt existing ones that have become popular in partnership literature (Matthews, Cook-Sather et al. 2019), and use a range of methodologies to further understand experiences, identify effects, and reveal associated mechanisms. The idea here is not to discredit or totally displace established and still evolving ways of theorizing partnership but rather never to let the theories become too static or so normalized that they are rendered invisible or automatic. Theories of partnership that advance equity and justice need to complicate, unsettle, or otherwise challenge thinking such that they prompt revision and action. One especially inspiring example, which we have mentioned earlier in the book, is the resituating of well-established underlying principles of partnership—"respect, reciprocity, and shared responsibility" (Cook-Sather, Bovill, and Felten 2014, 175)—in "the more explicitly feminist terms of agency, accountability, and affinity" (Cates, Madigan, and Reitenauer 2018, 37). Further theorizations can contribute to hermeneutical forms of epistemic justice—the creation of alternative tools for validating and making meaning of the experiences of partners from equity-seeking groups. Aspects of these experiences may otherwise remain uncovered when only drawing on the interpretive resources that have become established in partnership spaces.

The conceptual framework we develop over the course of this book has been focused on the impact of epistemic, affective, and ontological harms that constitute injustice to students from equity-seeking groups in postsecondary education, and the possibilities of partnership in offering redress. We have not yet highlighted in this discussion what this might mean, epistemically, affectively, and ontologically, for those working with these student partners, including staff and faculty partners and student partners from more privileged majority groups. For example, what would be required from those working with students from equity-seeking groups to affirm those students' disqualified knowledge? Fricker (2007) described this work to include becoming a responsible hearer, which involves proactively correcting for the prejudice one may hold that would otherwise prevent recognition of particular speakers or testimonies as legitimate knowers and knowledge. She explained: "What is needed on the part of the hearer in order to avert a testimonial injustice . . . is a corrective anti-prejudicial virtue that is distinctively *reflexive* in structure" (91). Participants are unlikely to enter partnership devoid of prejudices we have absorbed through our existence in dominant society. Working in partnership to advance equity and justice, then, must also involve grappling with these attitudes and beliefs we carry with us. Indeed, Fricker (2007) suggested that one way we can reduce our prejudicial judgments about the knowledge of others is through personal familiarity and habituation—such as getting to know our partners over the course of our work together.

Although we discussed in chapter 3 how pedagogical partnerships can contribute to enhanced confidence, empowerment, and other affective redress for students from historically marginalized groups, effecting a change—often a destabilizing one—in the emotions of faculty and staff partners and student partners who do not identify as belonging to equity-seeking groups is also vital to such redress. Partnership to advance equity and justice may not always feel "good" for those with relative privilege, and may require learning to sit with difficult emotions and challenges to strongly held beliefs:

> Discomfort . . . entails a particular ethic and a turbulent ground on which to critique deeply held assumptions about ourselves and others. . . . Some discomfort is not only unavoidable but may also be necessary for individual and social transformation (Berlak, 2004). (Zembylas 2017, 9)

Roselynn Verwoord, reflecting as a faculty partner on power in partnership relationships, wondered whether, "(despite my best intentions) I was taking on the role of the oppressor as a result of the positional power that I held in the partnership" (quoted in Kehler, Verwoord, and Smith 2017, 7). Heather Smith also offered some reflections on negotiating positionality in partnership:

> I've often had moments of surprise in my partnerships where I realized how deeply embedded I am in Western, masculinist norms and values. Working with Indigenous students and elders always provides me with moments of surprise about how colonial my practices can be. (Quoted in Verwoord and Smith 2020, 36)

Posing, reflecting on, and unpacking questions like this about power in partnership processes, which Kehler, Verwoord, and Smith (2017) and Verwoord and Smith (2020) have demonstrated and have encouraged us to do more often, generates necessary and important discomfort and uncertainty.

Those in more privileged positions can personally "benefit" from engaging in equity and justice work to support others as it can garner respect and increase one's reputation to be seen as someone "who 'get[s] it'" or "who at least trie[s]" (Patton and Bondi 2015, 506; also see Slater 2019). Ontologically, then, we also need to confront particular senses of selves and identities—the White savior, nice guy, good White person, good teacher, teacher hero, caring educator, social justice ally (Bryan 2016; Patton and Bondi 2015; Sharp-Hoskins and Robillard 2012; Slater 2019; Smith 2015), and other stories we are attached to and tell about who we are as partners, which can work to maintain whiteness, heteronormativity (e.g., gendered ideals of caring), and other oppressive social norms. We instead need to examine uncomfortable identities of complicity (e.g., as settler-colonizers, beneficiaries of enslavement) and open ourselves to having our worldview and sense of self interrupted:

> A willingness to engage in in-depth critical inquiry regarding systems of domination needs to be accompanied by a parallel of emotional willingness to engage in the difficult work of possibly allowing one's worldviews to be shattered. (Boler 2004, 128, quoted in Bryan 2016, 27)

As much as equity and justice work through partnership can affirm new ontological possibilities for student partners from equity-seeking groups, it may also disrupt, in vital ways, the ontological security of privileged positions.

## What Are Some Ways of Sustaining Ourselves in the Challenging Work of Promoting Equity and Justice Through Partnership?

We have discussed the ways in which partnership work can be taxing and emotionally draining for student partners, but by and large student partners describe the work as energizing and sustaining because it supports gaining perspective, doing meaningful work, being affirmed and listened to, and experiencing a sense of capacity and efficacy (Jonsson, forthcoming). As Perez-Putnam (2016) has noted, when she arrived at Haverford College, she "felt out of the loop, uninvolved, small, superfluous," but working in partnership made her feel that what she was doing was "important and would have a lasting impact," which contributed to her "deepening connection to the school" (1). It also gave her energy to feel that not only was she "working with this specific professor in the moment but also towards a far-away future Haverford in which all professors have had the same opportunity to think about their pedagogy within the space of the SaLT program" (1). In contrast to so much of the violence and harm we described in chapter 2 of this book that discounts and dismisses student identities, experiences, and perspectives, being affirmed and listened to shows recognition and valuing of those aspects and allows students to sustain themselves in this work. These student reflections suggest that the more that partnership enhances equity and justice (redresses harm), the more it energizes and sustains those involved. Therefore, advancing equity and justice are conditions of sustainability.

For these reasons, we recommend giving consideration to how to support and note these energizing experiences. Even, perhaps especially, when student partners are wrestling with challenging pedagogical issues, encountering resistance, or feeling the strain of the emotional labor of this work, those working with student partners can play an intentional and vital role in affirming students and their perspectives (Cook-Sather and Felten 2017b) and making space for and offering prompts to invite reflection on what makes the work energizing and thereby both more rewarding and more sustainable (Cook-Sather, Bahti, and Ntem 2019). It can also be energizing for student partners to connect across institutions, as student partners from nine different institutions did when the COVID-19 pandemic prompted colleges and universities to move online, and a student partner at one institution took the initiative and asked Alison to convene such a virtual gathering (Bala, forthcoming). Sharing perceptions of and strategies for how to attend to equity and justice when structural disadvantages were thrown into particular relief, student partners commented on the power of this suddenly emergent, intercollegiate partnership community.

These reflections on sustaining participants through the potentially difficult work of contributing to equity and justice via partnership underscore the value of nurturing and supporting community and connection among those involved in equity- and justice-focused partnerships. Just as opportunities to connect with others engaged in and open to partnership have been positioned as a helpful means of supporting individuals in the countercultural work of partnership more broadly (Brost et al. 2018; Marquis, Guitman et al. 2019; Ntem 2020), so too can the development of cohorts of students and faculty or staff, whether through programs or as an emergent collective of individual participants, help to sustain and energize those working on equity and justice through partnership (Cook-Sather, Bahti, and Ntem 2019; Marquis, Carrasco-Acosta et al. 2019; Ntem and Cook-Sather 2018). In addition to providing needed affirmation, connections with others engaged in similar work can offer participants a sense of "camaraderie and shared purpose" (Reckson 2014, 1), as well as opportunities to share strategies, ideas, and experiences (including both successes and challenges) that can support their equity and justice work.

In addition, we might encourage our student partners from equity-seeking groups to connect with student-led networks and community spaces as important sources of epistemic, affective, and ontological support during their partnership work, and consider compensating some of this time. Such spaces can affirm and develop students' minoritized cultural knowledge, skills, and networks instead of teaching them to assimilate into the university; deepen commitments to equity-seeking students as a group; and promote capacities to challenge social and institutional norms (Maldonado, Rhoads, and Buenavista 2005; Rhoads, Buenavista, and Maldonado 2004).

Writing as a Mad student partner, Alise (de Bie 2020) has also proposed skepticism and distrust as ways of engaging with pedagogical partnerships when the notion of partnership is not universally endorsed as a positive strategy in one's communities of affiliation. Such states may, for some, offer another kind of sustenance by affirming the commitments that partners from equity-seeking groups may hold to other community values and priorities, and leaving space for uncertainty regarding the strategy of partnership across difference.

Finally, scholars who focus on partnership work can be vigilant about ensuring that there are spaces and supports for students from equity-seeking groups to share their experiences and analyses, such as by drawing on their conceptual frames in coauthored pieces (de Bie et al. 2019; Ntem and Cook-Sather 2018), encouraging students to author work without staff and faculty partners (e.g., Colón García 2017; Perez-Putnam 2016; Yahlnaaw 2019), and further legitimizing this scholarship through our citation practices, as we have aimed to do throughout this book. We might also challenge the norms of venues such as conferences, as Alise recommended in chapter 6, and support students in delivering coauthored and solo presentations at conferences and institutes (e.g., Ntem 2017). These types of practices can be particularly vital for sustaining passion and motivation to advance equity and justice through partnership.

## Further Considerations: Reviewing Recommendations for Partnership in Relation to Equity and Justice

There is a rapidly expanding body of literature and set of resources that address questions of what is needed to make partnership work successful and how partnership initiatives might be facilitated and supported (e.g., Cook-Sather, Bahti, and Ntem 2019; Cook-Sather, Bovill, and Felten 2014; Curran and Millard 2016; Marquis, Black, and Healey 2017; Marquis, Guitman et al. 2019; Matthews, Mercer-Mapstone et al. 2019). To synthesize and build on the recommendations we have offered, we revisit two such resources here. Just as Cates, Madigan, and Reitenauer (2018) respectfully reframed "respect, reciprocity, and shared responsibility" (Cook-Sather, Bovill, and Felten 2014, 175) as "agency, accountability, and affinity" (37), we resituate these existing recommendations within our more specifically equity- and justice-focused frame. In so doing, we extend the process, which we began in chapters 3 and 4, of rereading partnership literature and practice in relation to our conceptual framework and offer a set of overarching considerations for those interested in working toward equity and justice through pedagogical partnership.

A set of general recommendations for developing a partnership program, such as that offered by Cook-Sather, Bahti, and Ntem (2019) in their online resource called "Checklist for Developing a Pedagogical Partnership Program," might be reframed in equity and justice terms and also adapted for those considering smaller-scale partnership initiatives, as we have done in the following list (the original recommendations are in regular font, the reframing in italics):

- Consider why you want to develop a pedagogical partnership program and what might get in the way, *paying particular attention to who has been well- and underserved by your institution, who stands to benefit from a partnership program or project (e.g., the institution, those least served), and what potential harm a partnership initiative might inadvertently cause.*
- Decide what kind of partnership program is right for your context *and how, in particular, such a program or project might redress harms and support the pursuit of greater equity and justice.*
- Think through how to situate and structure the program, get started, and plan for sustainability, *such that the needs and interests of those who have been least well served by the institution continue to be addressed in the program or project.*
- Decide on the shared responsibilities of facilitating pedagogical partnerships, *paying particular attention to the forms of and whose emotional as well as epistemic labor might be involved and how to resist emotional and epistemic exploitation.*
- Create an approach to inviting and supporting participants, *particularly attending to creating structures and approaches that welcome students from equity-seeking groups and recognize differences in experiences rather than assuming a homogeneous student perspective or experience.*
- Prepare for managing logistical and emotional challenges of partnership *and how differently positioned people will face different challenges, understanding that the challenges may not be fairly distributed and that participants will be differently impacted or affected by them.*
- Develop ways to assess pedagogical partnership work *that focus in particular on the potential for partnership to exacerbate or redress epistemic, affective, and ontological harms.*

As another, slightly more extended example, Matthews (2017) has argued that good partnership practice should aspire to (a) foster inclusive partnerships, (b) nurture power-sharing relationships through dialogue and reflection, (c) accept partnership as a process with uncertain outcomes, (d) engage in ethical partnerships, and (e) enact partnership for transformation. Several of these already have an explicit equity focus that could be extended and others could be reframed to foreground such a focus. In discussing the first principle, foster inclusive partnerships, Matthews (2017) offered several examples of partnership work that have embraced a focus on equity and inclusion, and she argued that institutions need to "direct attention to the experiences of a diversity of students as the focus of partnership work," while, at the same time, offer "a plethora of partnership opportunities that specifically seek to include students and staff from all backgrounds in meaningful, power-sharing learning partnerships that shape the university" (3). We might build on this general recommendation to suggest that directors of partnership programs and individuals planning to engage in partnership seek and invite students, faculty, and staff with particular equity-related concerns and areas of interest, such as Leslie's in epistemic violence and decolonizing practices, and create paid opportunities to pursue projects focused on these concerns. In addition, we recommend specifically inviting students from equity-seeking groups, not just in "equal proportion" to majority students but with an explicit focus on employment equity and challenging the imbalance of opportunities in the academy. Creating a specific stream to support equity-focused partnership work acts on Matthews's (2017) argument and sends a strong message regarding justice as a goal.

Matthews (2017) likewise both reviewed some of the ways that nurturing power-sharing relationships through dialogue and reflection, her second principle, have been addressed in the partnership literature and urged reflection on power dynamics. Building on this general recommendation, we advocate for a more focused naming of the kinds of power dynamics at play in particular partnerships based on partners' specific social locations and how dimensions of identity intersect with institutional practices, local and larger contexts, and more. Verwoord and Smith (2020) have made a similar argument, presenting a framework that might help individuals reflect on power dynamics at play in their partnerships and specifically urging a consideration of partners' positionality and the possibility of ethnocentrism in this process.

Expanding on Matthews's (2017) third principle, accepting partnership as a process with uncertain outcomes, within an equity frame, we might want to dig more deeply into who can tolerate, afford, and benefit from what kinds of uncertainty and at what point in their development and whose personal and professional selves might be damaged or otherwise harmed by such a process-oriented approach. We might also want to wrestle with the ramifications of "accepting partnership as a process with uncertain outcomes" in the case of equity and justice. If this means "accepting" that partnership may not always achieve equity and justice as an uncertain outcome, we would suggest that this be something we refuse to accept, even though it may be true at times. Perhaps, in some circumstances, instead of accepting uncertain outcomes, we commit to the complex and ongoing struggle for action and change toward greater equity and justice (even if the outcomes remain uncertain and in need of perpetual attention).

Sustaining the focus on process, Matthews's (2017) fourth principle, engaging in ethical partnerships, "necessitates a process of power-sharing between all involved," includes "working together for good," and means "serving more than the individuals involved as [students as partners] is part of a broader movement for social good grounded in democratic principles" (5). These general commitments to greater equity can be further concretized by addressing relevant questions: What might "power sharing" mean in particular cultural contexts, such as those Kaur and Yong Bing (2020) and Chng (2019) have described while working in partnership in Malaysia and Singapore, respectively, or the settler colonial contexts of countries such as Australia, Canada, and the United States? For which and for whose good(s) are we working together? When are democratic principles insufficient to name and redress epistemic, affective, and ontological harms? And how might our pedagogical partnership work serve greater equity and justice beyond the particular individuals directly involved?

Finally, Matthews's (2017) fifth principle, enacting partnership for transformation, argues that "genuine partnership in learning and teaching is an act of resistance to the traditional, often implicit, but accepted, hierarchical structure" (6). Although partnership for equity and justice certainly resists such structures, how might it more proactively challenge, dismantle, and provide alternatives to not only hierarchical but also harmful structures? When we enact partnership for transformation, Matthews (2017) argued, we engage in "our own active reflection and ongoing dialogue with others" (6). How might such work be explicitly framed and guided by naming and redressing epistemic, affective, and ontological harms created and perpetuated by violences structured into postsecondary education, and how might conversation with others about the harms they have experienced and how they might be addressed be central to such dialogue?

The approach we have modeled is one of building on existing advice regarding partnership by inviting, making space for, and supporting greater specificity and posing more pointed questions about the epistemic, affective, and ontological dimensions of experience that can contribute to greater equity and justice. Beyond those we begin to ask here, further equity- and justice-focused conceptualizations and analyses will no doubt generate new questions not yet asked and make new spaces not yet imagined or created.

## Conclusion

This book has been largely theoretical (offering a new conceptual framework) and reflective (analyzing existing and promising practices); we offer a synthesis and vision that has yet to be formally or fully applied in practice. That is, we offer an understanding of partnership literature that groups it according to considerations of epistemic, affective, and ontological redress, while much of this literature on its own—including our own work in partnership to advance equity and justice—does not specifically use this characterization. Likewise, we reread our practices and propose new approaches within the conceptual framework we offer. We are excited to see applications of this work unfold—how the framework developed here might change the ways we talk about partnership; the ways we recruit students, staff, and faculty into partnership; the support we offer partners; the questions we ask in our research on partnership; and the critiques and challenges raised about partnership. We are likewise eager to learn how the framing offered here might be adapted, altered, or replaced by scholars and practitioners working in different contexts, and bringing to bear different knowledge, experiences, and perspectives. We hope others will take up this work as an invitation to further discussion, engagement, and action that might help make postsecondary education institutions more just and equitable places.

# Further Details on Unpublished Data

## Study 1

A research project conducted by Leslie Patricia Luqueño supported by a grant from The Arthur Vining Davis Foundations through the Pennsylvania Consortium of Liberal Arts Colleges.

### *Researcher*

Leslie Patricia Luqueño

### *Description of Study*

In the fall of 2018, with approval from Bryn Mawr College's Institutional Review Board (IRB), Leslie conducted 12 face-to-face interviews with students of color from Haverford and Bryn Mawr Colleges, specifically focusing on their experiences within classes that helped them explore their identities. Students represented a wide range of majors, class years, and identities, but they all shared having one or two meaningful courses that helped them feel more connected to their coursework. Among the experiences shared, students discussed topics such as developing relationships with professors of color, reading material written by scholars from underrepresented groups in academia, engaging in nonhegemonic discussion and assignment practices, and countering Eurocentric approaches to the humanities and social sciences. Following the interviews, Leslie has focused her analysis on how these types of courses can be healing for students of color, particularly because they exist as counterspaces from the White academic spaces Haverford and Bryn Mawr Colleges create. Leslie is working on an article discussing the results of this study, and quotations that will not be used in that publication have been included in this book.

## Study 2

A study of the experiences of students from equity-seeking groups at Bryn Mawr and Haverford Colleges and McMaster University.

## Coresearchers

Alison Cook-Sather, Alise de Bie, McMaster University student partner Srikripa Krishna Prasad, Leslie Patricia Luqueño, Beth Marquis, and former Bryn Mawr College student partner Anita Ntem.

## Description of Study

Responding to the growing body of work considering the relationships between student–faculty partnership and questions of equity and inclusion (much of which is referenced in this book) and with approval from the IRBs at Bryn Mawr College and McMaster University, this multi-institutional research study sought to explore how students who identify as members of equity-seeking groups perceive the capacity of partnership to contribute to equity in teaching and learning. Current and former student partners at Bryn Mawr and Haverford Colleges (n=33) and McMaster University (n=8) took part in face-to-face or online interviews that explored their perspectives about how participating in partnership affected them personally (e.g., their feelings of confidence, their relationships with faculty and other students), the challenges they experienced working in partnership (e.g., working across differences in social location, encountering resistance from their partners), and how their work with their faculty partners contributed to enhancing classroom and campus equity more broadly. Several publications drawing on data gathered for this project have been cited in this book (Cook-Sather 2018b; Cook-Sather et al. 2019; de Bie et al. 2019), as has one article that was recently accepted for publication (Marquis et al. forthcoming). Quotations referenced throughout this book as coming from Study 2 represent additional data from this study that have not been included in any of these other publications.

## Study 3

A study conducted on being Black and experiencing belonging through partnership at Bryn Mawr and Berea Colleges.

## Coresearchers

Alison Cook-Sather; a former Bryn Mawr College student partner who became the first postbaccalaureate fellow for partnerships at Berea College, Khadijah Seay; and director of the Center for Teaching and Learning at Berea College, Leslie Ortquist-Ahrens.

## *Description of Study*

This study responds to research indicating both that a sense of belonging is fundamental to students' engagement, persistence, and success in postsecondary education and that racism systematically works against Black students experiencing belonging, engagement, persistence, and success. Research also suggests, as we discuss extensively in this book, that participating in student–faculty pedagogical partnership can foster a sense of belonging, contribute to the development of culturally sustaining pedagogy, and redress some of the harms experienced by minoritized postsecondary students. To learn more about these phenomena in relation to Black female college students in particular, and with approval from the IRBs at Bryn Mawr College and Berea College, Alison, Khadijah, and Leslie used a conceptual framework informed by research on belonging, critical race theory, and intersectionality and a methodology informed by a Black-feminist and womanist research paradigm and Black girl cartography. The study analyzes responses to a survey completed by 12 Black female students at Berea, Bryn Mawr, and Haverford Colleges, focusing on how the students who responded to the survey describe perceiving, feeling, and engaging differently as a result of participating in pedagogical partnership.

*Note*: Portions of quotes in this book are also included in a manuscript that is currently under review (after a "revise and resubmit"—Cook-Sather & Seay 2020).

# REFERENCES

20 U.S. Code § 1087–56 - Job location and development programs, 1087–56 Job location and development programs § (1992). https://www.law.cornell.edu/uscode/text/20/1087-56

Abustan, Paulina. 2017. "Collectively Feeling: Honoring the Emotional Experiences of Queer and Transgender Student of Color Activists." In *Queer People of Color in Higher Education,* edited by Joshua Moon Johnson and Gabriel Javier, 31–56. Charlotte, NC: Information Age.

Academics for Black Survival and Wellness. 2020. *Home page.* https://www.academics4blacklives.com/

Acevedo, E. n.d. Afro-Latina. Poetics. http://www.acevedowrites.com/poetics

Ahmed, Sara. 2012. *On Being Included: Racism and Diversity in Institutional Life.* Durham, NC: Duke University Press.

Alizai, Hassina. 2017. "Impact of Islamophobia on Post-Secondary Muslim Students Attending Ontario Universities." Master's diss., University of Western Ontario.

Anderson, R. Kirk. 2019. "Toward Thick Responsiveness: Engaging Identity-Based Student Protest Movements." *The Journal of Higher Education* 90 (3): 402–426.

Arnold, Noelle Witherspoon, Emily R. Crawford, and Muhammad Khalifa. 2016. "Psychological Heuristics and Faculty of Color: Racial Battle Fatigue and Tenure/Promotion." *Journal of Higher Education* 87 (6): 890–919.

Austin, Ashley, Shelley L. Craig, Michael P. Dentato, Shirley Roseman, and Lauren McInroy. 2019. "Elucidating Transgender Students' Experiences of Microaggressions in Social Work Programs: Next Steps for Creating Inclusive Educational Contexts." *Social Work Education* 38 (7): 908–924.

Bala, Nandeeta. Forthcoming. "A STEPP Into Uncertainty: Pursuing Passions to Embrace Pedagogical Risks." *Teaching and Learning Together in Higher Education.*

Balch, Erica. 2019. "New Access Strategy to Help Underrepresented Students Find Pathways to McMaster." *McMaster Daily News,* February 27, 2019. https://dailynews.mcmaster.ca/articles/new-access-strategy-to-help-under-represented-students-find-pathways-to-mcmaster/

Barnett, Brooke, and Peter Felten, Eds. 2016. *Intersectionality in Action: A Guide for Faculty and Campus Leaders for Creating Inclusive Classrooms and Institutions.* Sterling, VA: Stylus.

Barrineau, Susanna, and Lakin Anderson. 2018. "Learning 'Betwixt and Between': Opportunities and Challenges for Student-Driven Partnership." *International Journal for Students as Partners* 2 (1): 16–32. https://doi.org/10.15173/ijsap.v2i1.3224

Bartky, Sandra Lee. 1990. *Femininity and Domination: Studies in the Phenomenology of Oppression.* London, UK: Psychology Press.

Baum, Sandy. 2019. "Rethinking Federal Work-Study: Incremental Reform Is Not Enough." Urban Institute. https://www.urban.org/sites/default/files/publication/100007/rethinking_federal_work_study_0.pdf

Baumeister, Roy F., and Mark R. Leary. 1995. "The Need to Belong: Desire for Interpersonal Attachments as a Fundamental Human Motivation." *Psychological Bulletin* 117 (3): 497–529.

Bell, Amani, Stephanie Barahona, and Bonnie Rose Stanway. 2020. "On the Edge. The Spaces Between Student-Staff Partnerships." In *The Power of Partnership: Students, Faculty, and Staff Revolutionizing Higher Education,* edited by Lucy Mercer-Mapstone and Sophia Abbot, 123–135. Elon, NC: Elon University Center for Engaged Learning. https://doi.org/10.36284/celelon.oa2

Berenstain, Nora. 2016. "Epistemic Exploitation." *Ergo, an Open Access Journal of Philosophy* 3 (2): 569–590. 10.3998/ergo.12405314.0003.022

Bergmark, Ulrika, and Susanne Westman. 2016. "Co-Creating Curriculum in Higher Education: Promoting Democratic Values and a Multidimensional View on Learning." *International Journal for Academic Development* 21 (1): 28–40.

Bindra, Gagandeep, Kirthika Easwaran, Lamia Firasta, Monika Hirsch, Aakriti Kapoor, Alexandra Sosnowski, Taleisha Stec-Marksman, and Gizem Vatansever. 2018. "Increasing Representation and Equity in Students as Partners Initiatives." *International Journal for Students as Partners* 2 (2): 10–15. https://doi.org/10.15173/ijsap.v2i2.3536

Black, Christine, and Rachel Guitman. 2018. "Reflections on Partnership." *International Institute of Students as Partners Connect* (blog), January 26, 2018. https://macblog.mcmaster.ca/summer-institute/2018/01/26/reflections-on-partnership/

Bohanon, Mariah. 2018. "Canadian Universities Band Together to Improve Diversity and Inclusion in Higher Education." Insight Into Diversity, May 15, 2018. https://www.insightintodiversity.com/canadian-universities-band-together-to-improve-diversity-and-inclusion-in-higher-education/

Bonilla-Silva, Eduardo. 2018. *Racism Without Racists: Color-Blind Racism and the Persistence of Racial Inequality in America.* Lanham, MD: Rowman & Littlefield.

Bovill, Catherine, Alison Cook-Sather, and Peter Felten. 2011. "Students as Co-Creators of Teaching Approaches, Course Design and Curricula: Implications for Academic Developers." *International Journal for Academic Development* 16 (2): 133–145.

Bovill, Catherine, Alison Cook-Sather, Peter Felten, Luke Millard, and Niamh Moore-Cherry. 2016. "Addressing Potential Challenges in Co-Creating Learning and Teaching: Overcoming Resistance, Navigating Institutional Norms and Ensuring Inclusivity in Student–Staff Partnerships." *Higher Education* 71 (2): 195–208.

Brost, Christel, Christelle Lauture, Karen Smith, and Saskia Kersten. 2018. "Reflections on That-Has-Been: Snapshots From the Students-as-Partners Movement." *International Journal for Students as Partners* 2 (1): 130–135. https://doi.org/10.15173/ijsap.v2i1.3366

Brown, Kate, Alise de Bie, Akshay Aggarwal, Ryan Joslin, Sarah Williams-Habibi, and Vipusaayini Sivanesanathan. 2020. "Students With Disabilities as Partners: A Case Study on User Testing an Accessibility Website." *International Journal for Students as Partners* 4 (2). https://doi.org/10.15173/ijsap.v4i2.4051

Brunson, Mary. 2018. "The Formation and Power of Trust: How It Was Created and Enacted Through Collaboration." *Teaching and Learning Together in Higher Education* 23. https://repository.brynmawr.edu/tlthe/vol1/iss23/2

Bryan, Audrey. 2016. "The Sociology Classroom as a Pedagogical Site of Discomfort: Difficult Knowledge and the Emotional Dynamics of Teaching and Learning." *Irish Journal of Sociology* 24 (1): 7–33.

Bryson, Colin, Ruth Furlonger, and Fae Rinaldo-Landridge. 2015. "A Critical Consideration of, and Research Agenda for, the Approach of 'Students as Partners.'" Paper presented at the 2015 International Conference on Improving University Teaching, Ljubljana, Slovenia, July. https://www.iutconference.com/2016/01/a-critical-consideration-of-and-research-agenda-for-the-approach-of-students-as-partners/

Burns, Tom, Sandra Sinfield, and Sandra Abegglen. 2019. "Third Space Partnerships With Students: Becoming Educational Together." *International Journal for Students as Partners* 3 (1): 60–68. https://doi.org/10.15173/ijsap.v3i1.3742

Cates, Rhiannon M., Mariah R. Madigan, and Vicki L. Reitenauer. 2018. "'Locations of Possibility': Critical Perspectives on Partnership." *International Journal for Students as Partners* 2 (1): 33–46. https://doi.org/10.15173/ijsap.v2i1.3341

Charkoudian, Louise K., Anna C. Bitners, Noah B. Bloch, and Saadia Nawal. 2015. "Dynamic Discussion and Informed Improvements: Student-Led Revision of First-Semester Organic Chemistry." *Teaching and Learning Together in Higher Education* 15. https://repository.brynmawr.edu/tlthe/vol1/iss15/5

Chávez, Alicia Fedelina, and Susan Diana Longerbeam. 2016. *Teaching Across Cultural Strengths: A Guide To Balancing Integrated and Individuated Cultural Frameworks in College Teaching.* Sterling, VA: Stylus.

Chen, Julie, and John Ho. 2020. "A Medical Humanities Curriculum in Medical School: Unexpected Partnerships and Unintended Consequences." In *Building Courage, Confidence, and Capacity in Learning and Teaching Through Student-Faculty Partnership: Stories From Across Contexts and Arenas of Practice,* edited by Alison Cook-Sather and Chanelle Wilson, 21–27. Lanham, MD: Lexington Books.

Chng, Huang Hoon. 2019. "The Possibilities of Students as Partners—A Perspective From Singapore." *Teaching and Learning Together in Higher Education* 27. https://repository.brynmawr.edu/tlthe/vol1/iss27/3/

Chukwu, Amarachi, and Kim Jones. 2020. "Feminist Interventions in Engineering: Co-Creating Across Disciplines and Identities." In *Building Courage, Confidence, and Capacity in Learning and Teaching Through Student-Faculty Partnership: Stories From Across Contexts and Arenas of Practice,* edited by Alison Cook-Sather and Chanelle Wilson, 11–20. Lanham, MD: Lexington Books.

Clark, D. Anthony, Sela Kleiman, Lisa B. Spanierman, Paige Isaac, and Gauthamie Poolokasingham. 2014. "'Do You Live in a Teepee?' Aboriginal Students'

Experiences with Racial Microaggressions in Canada." *Journal of Diversity in Higher Education* 7 (2): 112–125.

Coates, Ta-Nehisi. 2015. *Between the World and Me.* New York, NY: Spiegel & Grau.

Cohen, Geoffrey L., and Julio Garcia. 2008. "Identity, Belonging, and Achievement: A Model, Interventions, Implications." *Current Directions in Psychological Science* 17 (6): 365–369.

Cokley, Kevin, Shannon McClain, Alicia Enciso, and Mercedes Martinez. 2013. "An Examination of the Impact of Minority Status Stress and Impostor Feelings on the Mental Health of Diverse Ethnic Minority College Students." *Journal of Multicultural Counseling and Development* 41 (2): 82–95.

Collins, Ayse, Fara Azmat, and Ruth Rentschler. 2019. "'Bringing Everyone on the Same Journey': Revisiting Inclusion in Higher Education." *Studies in Higher Education* 44 (8): 1475–1487. https://doi.org/10.1080/03075079.2018.1450852

Colón García, Ana. 2017. "Building a Sense of Belonging Through Pedagogical Partnership." *Teaching and Learning Together in Higher Education* 22. http://repository.brynmawr.edu/tlthe/vol1/iss22/2

Conner, Jerusha. 2012. "Steps in Walking the Talk: How Working With a Student Consultant Helped Me Integrate Student Voice More Fully Into My Pedagogical Planning and Practice." *Teaching and Learning Together in Higher Education* 6. http://repository.brynmawr.edu/tlthe/vol1/iss6/6

Cook-Sather, Alison. 2006. "Production, Cure, or Translation? Rehumanizing Education and the Roles of Teacher and Student in US Schools and Universities." *FORUM: For Promoting 3–19 Comprehensive Education* 48 (3): 329–336.

Cook-Sather, Alison. 2014. "Student–Faculty Partnership in Explorations of Pedagogical Practice: A Threshold Concept in Academic Development." *International Journal for Academic Development* 19 (3): 186–198.

Cook-Sather, Alison. 2015. "Dialogue Across Differences of Position, Perspective, and Identity: Reflective Practice in/on a Student-Faculty Pedagogical Partnership Program." *Teachers College Record* 117 (2). https://repository.brynmawr.edu/cgi/viewcontent.cgi?article=1032&context=edu_pubs

Cook-Sather, Alison. 2016. "Undergraduate Students as Partners in New Faculty Orientation and Academic Development." *International Journal of Academic Development* 21 (2): 151–162.

Cook-Sather, Alison. 2018a. "Developing 'Students as Learners and Teachers': Lessons From Ten Years of Pedagogical Partnership That Strives to Foster Inclusive and Responsive Practice." *Journal of Educational Innovation, Partnership and Change* 4 (1). https://journals.gre.ac.uk/index.php/studentchangeagents/article/view/746

Cook-Sather, Alison. 2018b. "Listening to Equity-Seeking Perspectives: How Students' Experiences of Pedagogical Partnership Can Inform Wider Discussions of Student Success." *Higher Education Research and Development* 37 (5): 923–936.

Cook-Sather, Alison. 2018c. "Perpetual Translation: Conveying the Languages and Practices of Student Voice and Pedagogical Partnership Across Differences of Identity, Culture, Position, and Power." *Transformative Dialogues* 11 (3). http://

www.kpu.ca/sites/default/files/Transformative%20Dialogues/TD.11.3_Cook-Sather_Perpetual_Translation.pdf

Cook-Sather, Alison. 2019. "Increasing Inclusivity Through Pedagogical Partnerships Between Students and Faculty." *Diversity & Democracy* 22 (1). https://www.aacu.org/diversitydemocracy/2019/winter/cook-sather

Cook-Sather, Alison. 2020. "Respecting Voices: How the Co-Creation of Teaching and Learning Can Support Academic Staff, Underrepresented Students, and Equitable Practices." *Higher Education* 79 (5), 885–901.

Cook-Sather, Alison, and Sophia Abbot. 2016. "Translating Partnerships: How Faculty-Student Collaboration in Explorations of Teaching and Learning Can Transform Perceptions, Terms, and Selves." *Teaching & Learning Inquiry* 4 (2): 1–14. https://doi.org/10.20343/teachlearninqu.4.2.5

Cook-Sather, Alison, Sophia Abbot, and Peter Felten. 2019. "Legitimating Reflective Writing in SoTL: 'Dysfunctional Illusions of Rigor' Revisited." *Teaching & Learning Inquiry* 7 (2): 14–27. https://doi. org/10.20343/teachlearninqu.7.2.2

Cook-Sather, Alison, and Praise Agu. 2013. "Students of Color and Faculty Members Working Together Toward Culturally Sustaining Pedagogy." In *To Improve the Academy: Resources for Faculty, Instructional, and Organizational Development*, edited by James E. Groccia and Laura Cruz, 271–285. San Francisco, CA: Jossey-Bass/Anker.

Cook-Sather, Alison, and Zanny Alter. 2011. "What Is and What Can Be: How a Liminal Position Can Change Learning and Teaching in Higher Education." *Anthropology & Education Quarterly* 42 (1): 37–53.

Cook-Sather, Alison, Melanie Bahti, and Anita Ntem. 2019. *Pedagogical Partnerships: A How-To Guide for Faculty, Students, and Academic Developers in Higher Education*. Elon, NC: Elon University Center for Engaged Learning. https://doi.org/10.36284/celelon.oa1

Cook-Sather, Alison, and Nandeeta Bala. 2020. "Naming and Navigating Troubling Transitions: Pedagogical Partnership During the Pandemic." *Teaching and Learning Together in Higher Education* 30. https://repository.brynmawr.edu/tlthe/vol1/iss30/1/

Cook-Sather, Alison, Catherine Bovill, and Peter Felten. 2014. *Engaging Students as Partners in Learning and Teaching: A Guide for Faculty*. San Francisco, CA: Jossey-Bass.

Cook-Sather, Alison, and Crystal Des-Ogugua. 2019. "Lessons We Still Need to Learn on Creating More Inclusive and Responsive Classrooms: Recommendations From One Student-Faculty Partnership Program." *International Journal of Inclusive Education* 23 (6): 594–608.

Cook-Sather, Alison, Crystal Des-Ogugua, and Melanie Bahti. 2018. "Articulating Identities and Analyzing Belonging: A Multistep Intervention That Affirms and Informs a Diversity of Students." *Teaching in Higher Education* 23 (3): 374–389.

Cook-Sather, Alison, and Peter Felten. 2017a. "Ethics of Academic Leadership: Guiding Learning and Teaching." In *Cosmopolitan Perspectives on Becoming an Academic Leader in Higher Education*, edited by Feng Su and Margaret Wood, 175–191. London, UK: Bloomsbury.

Cook-Sather, Alison, and Peter Felten. 2017b. "Where Student Engagement Meets Faculty Development: How Student-Faculty Pedagogical Partnership Fosters a Sense of Belonging." *Student Engagement in Higher Education Journal* 1 (2): 3–11. https://journals.gre.ac.uk/index.php/raise/article/view/cook

Cook-Sather, Alison, Launa Gauthier, and Miciah Foster. 2020. "The Role of Growth Mindset in Developing Pedagogical Partnership Programs: Findings From a Cross-Institutional Study." *Journal of Innovation, Partnership and Change* 6, 1. https://journals.studentengagement.org.uk/index.php/studentchangeagents/article/view/1004

Cook-Sather, Alison, Srikripa Krishna Prasad, Elizabeth Marquis, and Anita Ntem. 2019. "Mobilizing a Culture Shift on Campus: Underrepresented Students as Educational Developers." *New Directions for Teaching and Learning* 2019 (159): 21–30.

Cook-Sather, Alison, and Brook Lillehaugen. 2020, January. "Navigating and Transforming Higher Education: A Co-Curricular, Co-Created Approach to Fostering Student Success and Institutional Culture Change." Presentation at the Conference of the Association of American Colleges & Universities, Washington DC, 22–25.

Cook-Sather, Alison, and Alia Luz. 2015. "Greater Engagement in and Responsibility for Learning: What Happens When Students Cross the Threshold of Student–Faculty Partnership." *Higher Education Research & Development* 34 (6): 1097–1109.

Cook-Sather, Alison, Kelly E. Matthews, Anita Ntem, and Sandra Leathwick. 2018. "What We Talk About When We Talk About Students as Partners." *International Journal for Students as Partners* 2 (2): 1–9. https://doi.org/10.15173/ijsap.v2i2.3790

Cook-Sather, Alison, and Yeidaly Mejia. 2018. "Students Experience Empowerment and Empathy Through Pedagogical Partnership." *British Educational Research Association Blog,* July 20, 2018. https://www.bera.ac.uk/blog/students-experience-empowerment-and-empathy-through-pedagogical-partnership

Cook-Sather, Alison, Leslie Ortquist-Ahrens, and Bill Reynolds. 2019. "Building Belonging Through Pedagogical Partnership: Connecting Within and Across Institutions." Presentation at the Professional and Organizational Development Network Conference, Pittsburgh, PA, November 13–17.

Cook-Sather, Alison, and Olivia Porte. 2017. "Reviving Humanity: Grasping Within and Beyond Our Reach." *Journal of Educational Innovation, Partnership and Change* 3 (1). https://journals.gre.ac.uk/index.php/studentchangeagents/article/view/638

Cook-Sather, Alison, Joel Schlosser, Abigail Sweeney, Laurel Peterson, Kimberly Cassidy, and Ana Colón García. 2017. "The Pedagogical Benefits of Enacting Positive Psychology Practices Through a Student-Faculty Partnership Approach to Academic Development." *International Journal for Academic Development* 23 (2): 123–134.

Cook-Sather, Alison, and Khadijah Seay. 2020. "'I Was Involved as an Equal Member of the Community': How Pedagogical Partnership Can Foster a Sense of Belonging in Black, Female Students." Unpublished manuscript (under review).

Cook-Sather, Alison, Helen White, Tomás Aramburu, Camille Samuels, and Paul Wynkoop. 2020. "Moving Toward Greater Equity and Inclusion in STEM Through Pedagogical Partnership." In *Transforming Institutions: Accelerating Systemic Change in Higher Education,* edited by Andrea Beach, Charles Henderson, Noah Finkelstein, Scott Simkins, Gabriela Weaver, and Kate White. Montreal, QC: Pressbooks. http://openbooks.library.umass.edu/assscnti2020/

Corbin, Kathryne Adair, and Carol Lee Diallo. 2019. "Striving To Make French and Francophone Studies More Inclusive." *Teaching and Learning Together in Higher Education*    28.    https://repository.brynmawr.edu/cgi/viewcontent.cgi?article=1221&context=tlthe

Curran, Roisín, and Luke Millard. 2016. "A Partnership Approach to Developing Student Capacity to Engage and Staff Capacity to Be Engaging: Opportunities for Academic Developers." *International Journal for Academic Development* 21 (1): 67–78.

Daddow, Angela. 2016. "Curricula and Pedagogic Potentials When Educating Diverse Students in Higher Education: Students' Funds of Knowledge as a Bridge to Disciplinary Learning." *Teaching in Higher Education* 21 (7): 741–758.

Daly, James. 2000. "Marx and Justice." *International Journal of Philosophical Studies* 8 (3): 351–370.

Daniel, Beverly-Jean. 2019. "Teaching While Black: Racial Dynamics, Evaluations, and the Role of White Females in the Canadian Academy in Carrying the Racism Torch." *Race, Ethnicity and Education* 22 (1): 21–37.

de Bie, Alise. 2019a. "Living a Mad Politics: Affirming Mad Onto-Ethico-Epistemologies Through Resonance, Resistance, and Relational Redress of Epistemic-Affective Harm." PhD diss., McMaster University.

de Bie, Alise. 2019b. "Finding Ways (and Words) to Move: Mad Student Politics and Practices of Loneliness." *Disability & Society* 34 (7–8). https://doi.org/10.1080/09687599.2019.1609910

de Bie, Alise. 2020. "Respectfully Distrusting 'Students as Partners' Practice in Higher Education: Applying a Mad Politics of Partnership." *Teaching in Higher Education,* March 9, 2020, 1–21. https://doi.org/10.1080/13562517.2020.1736023

de Bie, Alise, and Kate Brown. 2017. "Forward with FLEXibility: A Teaching and Learning Resource on Accessibility and Inclusion." MacPherson Institute, McMaster University. https://flexforward.pressbooks.com/

de Bie, Alise, Janice Chaplin, Jennie Vengris, Eminet Dagnachew, and Randy Jackson. 2020 November 12: 1–17. "Not 'Everything's a Learning Experience': Racialized, Indigenous, 2SLGBTQ, and Disabled Students in Social Work Field Placements." *Social Work Education.* https://doi.org/10.1080/02615479.2020.1843614

de Bie, Alise, Shaila Kumbhare, Jessica Evans, and Sarah Mantini. 2017. "Parting From Partnership to Enable Future Collaboration: Disabled Student Perspectives." Presentation at MacPherson Institute's 2017 Research on Teaching and Learning Conference, McMaster University, Hamilton, ON, November.

de Bie, Alise, Elizabeth Marquis, Alison Cook-Sather, and Leslie Luqueño. 2019. "Valuing Knowledge(s) and Cultivating Confidence: Contributing to Epistemic

Justice via Student-Faculty Pedagogical Partnerships." In *International Perspectives in Higher Education: Strategies for Fostering Inclusive Classrooms*, edited by Jaimie Hoffman, Patrick Blessinger, and Mandla Makhanya, 35–48. Bingley, UK: Emerald Publishing.

de Bie, Alise, and Rille Raaper. 2019. "Troubling the Idea of Partnership." *International Institute on Students as Partners Connect* (blog), March 29, 2019. https://macblog. mcmaster.ca/summer-institute/2019/03/29/troubling-the-idea-of-partnership/

del Carmen Salazar, Maria. 2013. "A Humanizing Pedagogy: Reinventing the Principles and Practice of Education as a Journey Toward Liberation." *Review of Research in Education* 37 (1): 121–148.

Delgado Bernal, Dolores. 2002. "Critical Race Theory, Latino Critical Theory, and Critical Raced-Gendered Epistemologies: Recognizing Students of Color as Holders and Creators of Knowledge." *Qualitative Inquiry* 8 (1): 105–126.

Devlin, Marcia. 2013. "Bridging Socio-Cultural Incongruity: Conceptualising the Success of Students From Low Socio-Economic Status Backgrounds in Higher Education." *Studies in Higher Education* 38 (6): 939–949.

Dillon, Robin S. 1997. "Self-Respect: Moral, Emotional, Political." *Ethics* 107 (2): 226–249.

Doran, John, Amanda K. Ferguson, Gulam A. Khan, Grace A. Ryu, Dominic Naimool, Mark D. Hanson, and Ruth A. Childs. 2015. "What Are Ontario's Universities Doing to Improve Access for Under-Represented Groups?" Toronto, ON: HEQCO. https://heqco.ca/pub/what-are-ontarios-universities-doing-to-improve-access-for-under-represented-groups/

Doyle, Robyn, and Usha George. 2008. "Achieving and Measuring Diversity: An Organizational Change Approach." *Social Work Education* 27 (1): 97–110.

Dunne, Elisabeth, and Roos Zandstra. 2011. *Students as Change Agents. New Ways of Engaging With Learning and Teaching in Higher Education*. Bristol, UK: ESCalate, Higher Education Academy Subject Centre for Education, University of Exeter. http://escalate.ac.uk/8064

Dwyer, Alexander. 2018. "Toward the Formation of Genuine Partnership Spaces." *International Journal for Students as Partners* 2 (1): 11–15. https://doi.org/ 10.15173/ijsap.v2i1.3503

Elaneh, Elias. 2019. "Re-Evaluating Motivation: Learning From the Fourth Annual Student Partners Symposium." *International Institute on Students as Partners* (blog), June 27, 2019. https://macblog.mcmaster.ca/summer-institute/2019/06/27/re-evaluating -motivation-learning-from-the-fourth-annual-student-partners-symposium/

Elias, Michael. 2019. "Task Force on Student Work & Service: Spring 2019 Report." Haverford, PA: Haverford College.

Equity and Inclusion Office. 2017. "Report on the Challenging Islamophobia on Campus Initiative: December 2015–May 2016." McMaster University. https:// equity.mcmaster.ca/documents/challenging-islamophobia-on-campus-initiative-report-2015-2016.docx

Eze, Amaka. 2019. "From Listening to Responding to Leading: Building Capacity Through Four Pedagogical Partnerships." *Teaching and Learning Together in Higher Education* 26. https://repository.brynmawr.edu/tlthe/vol1/iss26/2

Felten, Peter. 2017. "Emotion and Partnerships." *International Journal for Students as Partners* 1 (2). https://doi.org/10.15173/ijsap.v1i2.3070

Felten, Peter, Julianne Bagg, Michael Bumbry, Jennifer Hill, Karen Hornsby, Maria Pratt, and Saranne Weller. 2013. "A Call for Expanding Inclusive Student Engagement in SoTL." *Teaching and Learning Inquiry* 1 (2): 63–74.

Filion-Murphy, Christine, Lindsey Hands, Lindsey Hockham, Laura Kirkpatrick, Sinead McNamara, Alison Strath, Iaian Rowe, and Helen Vosper. 2015. "Student-Led Development and Evaluation of a Community Pharmacy-Based Cardiovascular Risk Assessment." *Journal of Educational Innovation, Partnership and Change* 1 (2). http://dx.doi.org/10.21100/jeipc.v1i2.176

Fine, Michelle. 2015. "Resisting Whiteness/Bearing Witness." In *Everyday White People Confront Racial and Social Injustice*, edited by Eddie Moore Jr., Marguerite W. Penick-Parks, and Paul C. Gorski, 162–169. Sterling, VA: Stylus.

Fletcher, Joan, Claudia Bernard, Anna Fairtlough, and Akile Ahmet. 2013. "Beyond Equal Access to Equal Outcomes: The Role of the Institutional Culture in Promoting Full Participation, Positive Inter-Group Interaction and Timely Progression for Minority Social Work Students." *British Journal of Social Work* 45 (1): 120–137.

Follwell, Tianna-Lynn, Alan Santinele Martino, and Elizabeth Marquis. 2018. "Teaching at the Intersections: Identity, Social Location, and the Experiences of Teaching Assistants." Presentation at the McMaster Research on Teaching and Learning Conference, Hamilton, ON, December 12–13.

Franklin, Jeremy D., William A. Smith, and Man Hung. 2014. "Racial Battle Fatigue for Latina/o Students: A Quantitative Perspective." *Journal of Hispanic Higher Education* 13 (4): 303–322.

Fraser, Jennifer, Moonisah Usman, Kate Carruthers Thomas, Mayed Ahmed, Anna Dolidze, Fathimath Zuruwath Zareer, Rumy Begum, Bradley Elliott, and Evgeniya Macleod. 2020. "'I've Seen You': A Conversation About the Transformative Potential of Working in Partnership." In *The Power of Partnership: Students, Faculty, and Staff Revolutionizing Higher Education,* edited by Lucy Mercer-Mapstone and Sophia Abbot, 205–219. Elon, NC: Elon University Center for Engaged Learning. https://doi.org/10.36284/celelon.oa2

Fricker, Miranda. 2007. *Epistemic Injustice: Power and the Ethics of Knowing.* Oxford, UK: Oxford University Press.

Friedler, Delilah. 2020. "Obama Sees Hope in Protests: 'There Is Something Different Here.'" *Mother Jones,* June 3, 2020. https://www.motherjones.com/crime-justice/2020/06/obama-sees-hope-in-protests-there-is-something-different-here/

Gaston, Paul L. 2018. "Something Happened: What Was Once a Smooth Path for the Higher Education Act Has Become a Rocky Road." *Change: The Magazine of Higher Learning* 50 (3–4): 119–123. https://doi.org/10.1080/00091383.2018.1509641

Gay, Geneva. 2002. "Preparing for Culturally Responsive Teaching." *Journal of Teacher Education* 53 (2): 106–116.

Gennocro, Angela, and John Straussberger. 2020. "Peers and Colleagues: Collaborative Class Design Through Student-Faculty Partnerships." In *Building Courage, Confidence, and Capacity in Learning and Teaching Through Student-Faculty Partnership: Stories From Across Contexts and Arenas of Practice,* edited by Alison Cook-Sather and Chanelle Wilson, 29–37. Lanham, MD: Lexington Books.

George, Usha, Wes Shera, and A. Kah Tat Tsang. 1998. "Responding to Diversity in Organizational Life: The Case of a Faculty of Social Work." *International Journal of Inclusive Education* 2 (1): 73–86.

Gibson, Suanne. 2015. "When Rights Are Not Enough: What Is? Moving Towards New Pedagogy for Inclusive Education within UK Universities." *International Journal of Inclusive Education* 19 (8): 875–886.

Gibson, Suanne, and Alison Cook-Sather. 2020. "Politicised Compassion and Pedagogical Partnership." *International Journal for Students as Partners* 4 (1). https://doi.org/10.15173/ijsap.v4i1.3996

Glauser, Wendy. 2018. "Universities Make Way for the 'Non-Traditional' Student." *University Affairs,* August 1, 2018. https://www.universityaffairs.ca/features/feature-article/make-way-for-the-non-traditional-student/

Goldsmith, Meredith, and Nicole Gervasio. 2011. "Radical Equality: A Dialogue on Building a Partnership—and a Program—Through a Cross-Campus Collaboration." *Teaching and Learning Together in Higher Education* 3. http://repository.brynmawr.edu/tlthe/vol1/iss3/4

Gonzales, Lauren, Kristin C. Davidoff, Kevin L. Nadal, and Philip T. Yanos. 2015. "Microaggressions Experienced by Persons With Mental Illnesses: An Exploratory Study." *Psychiatric Rehabilitation Journal* 38 (3): 234–241.

Gonzales, Leslie D. 2015. "An Acción Approach to Affirmative Action: Hispanic-Serving Institutions as Spaces for Fostering Epistemic Justice." *Association of Mexican American Educators Journal* 9 (1): 28–41. http://amaejournal.utsa.edu/index.php/amae/article/view/249

Gopalan, Maithreyi, and Shannon T. Brady. 2019. "College Students' Sense of Belonging: A National Perspective." *Educational Researcher* 49 (2): 134–137. https://doi.org/10.3102/0013189X19897622

Government of Canada. 2019. "Dimensions: Equity, Diversity and Inclusion Canada." http://www.nserc-crsng.gc.ca/NSERC-CRSNG/EDI-EDI/Dimensions-Charter_Dimensions-Charte_eng.asp

Green, Wendy Jeannette. 2019. "Stretching the Cultural-Linguistic Boundaries of 'Students as Partners.'" *International Journal for Students as Partners* 3 (1): 84–88. https://doi.org/10.15173/ijsap.v3i1.3791

Guitman, Rachel, Anita Acai, and Lucy Mercer-Mapstone. 2020. "Unlearning Hierarchies and Striving for Relational Diversity. A Feminist Manifesto for Student-Staff Partnerships." In *The Power of Partnership: Students, Faculty, and Staff Revolutionizing Higher Education,* edited by Lucy Mercer-Mapstone and Sophia Abbot, 61–72. Elon, NC: Elon University Center for Engaged Learning. https://doi.org/10.36284/celelon.oa2

Guitman, Rachel, and Elizabeth Marquis. 2020. "A Radical Practice? Considering the Relationships Between Partnership and Social Change." In *The Power of*

*Partnership: Students, Faculty, and Staff Revolutionizing Higher Education,* edited by Lucy Mercer-Mapstone and Sophia Abbot, 137–150. Elon, NC: Elon University Center for Engaged Learning. https://doi.org/10.36284/celelon.oa2

Hanasono, Lisa K., Ellen M. Broido, Margaret M. Yacobucci, Karen V. Root, Susana Peña, and Deborah A. O'Neil. 2019. "Secret Service: Revealing Gender Biases in the Visibility and Value of Faculty Service." *Journal of Diversity in Higher Education* 12 (1): 85–98.

Harper, Brian E. 2019. "African American Access to Higher Education: The Evolving Role of Historically Black Colleges and Universities." *American Academic* 3, 109–128. https://academic.csuohio.edu/harper_b/AFrican_American_access.pdf

Harper, Shaun R., and Charles H. F. Davis III. 2016. "Eight Actions to Reduce Racism in College Classrooms." American Association of University Professors. https://www.aaup.org/comment/3881#.WhTRGbT81E5

Harper, Shaun, Lori D. Patton, and Ontario S. Wooden. 2009. "Access and Equity for African American Students in Higher Education: A Critical Race Historical Analysis of Policy Efforts." *The Journal of Higher Education* 80 (4): 389–414. https://doi.org/10.1080/00221546.2009.11779022

Haynie, Aeron. 2018. "Equity-Minded Faculty Development." *To Improve the Academy* 37 (1): 55–62.

Healey, Mick, Abbi Flint, and Kathy Harrington. 2014. *Engagement Through Partnership: Students as Partners in Learning and Teaching in Higher Education.* York, UK: Higher Education Academy.

Healey, Mick, Abbi Flint, and Kathy Harrington. 2016. "Students as Partners: Reflections on a Conceptual Model." *Teaching and Learning Inquiry* 4 (2): 1–13. tlijournal.com/tli/index.php/TLI/issue/view/15/

Healey, Mick, and Ruth L. Healey. 2018. "'It Depends': Exploring the Context-Dependent Nature of Students as Partners Practices and Policies." *International Journal for Students as Partners* 2 (1): 1–10. https://doi.org/10.15173/ijsap.v2i1.3472

Healey, Mick, Kelly E. Matthews, and Alison Cook-Sather. 2020. *Writing About Learning and Teaching in Higher Education: Creating and Contributing to Scholarly Conversations Across a Range of Genres.* Elon, NC: Elon University Center for Engaged Learning. https://doi.org/10.36284/celelon.oa3

Healey, Ruth L., Mick Healey, and Anthony Cliffe. 2018. "Engaging In Radical Work: Students as Partners in Academic Publishing." *Efficiency Exchange* (blog), May 1, 2018. http://www.efficiencyexchange.ac.uk/12775/engaging-radical-work-students-partners-academic-publishing/

Healey, Ruth, Alex Lerczak, Katharine Welsh, and Derek France. 2019. "By Any Other Name? The Impacts of Differing Assumptions, Expectations, and Misconceptions in Bringing About Resistance to Student-Staff Partnership." *International Journal for Students as Partners* 3 (1): 106–122. https://doi.org/10.15173/ijsap.v3i1.3cite0

Henry, Frances, Enakshi Dua, Audrey Kobayashi, Carl James, Peter Li, Howard Ramos, and Malinda S. Smith. 2017. "Race, Racialization and Indigeneity in Canadian Universities." *Race Ethnicity and Education* 20 (3): 300–314.

Hermsen, Tara, Thomas Kuiper, Frits Roelofs, and Joost van Wijchen. 2017. "Without Emotions, Never a Partnership!" *International Journal for Students as Partners* 1 (2). https://doi.org/10.15173/ijsap.v1i2.3228

Hipolito-Delgado, Carlos P. 2010. "Exploring the Etiology of Ethnic Self-Hatred: Internalized Racism in Chicana/o and Latina/o College Students." *Journal of College Student Development* 51 (3): 319–331.

Ho, Elizabeth. 2017. "Small Steps Toward an Ethos of Partnership in a Hong Kong University: Lessons From a Focus Group on 'Homework.'" *International Journal for Students as Partners* 1 (2). https://doi.org/10.15173/ijsap.v1i2.3198

Hoffman, Garrett D., and Tania D. Mitchell. 2016. "Making Diversity 'Everyone's Business': A Discourse Analysis of Institutional Responses to Student Activism for Equity and Inclusion." *Journal of Diversity in Higher Education* 9 (3): 277–289.

Howell, Annie, and Frank Tuitt, Eds. 2003. *Race and Higher Education: Rethinking Pedagogy in Diverse College Classrooms.* Cambridge, MA: Harvard Educational Review.

Huijser, Henk, James Wilson, Yao Wu, Shuang Qiu, Kangxin Wang, Shun Li, Wenye Chen, and M.B.N. Kouwenhoven. 2019. "Putting Student Partnership and Collaboration Centre-Stage in a Research-Led Context." *International Journal for Students as Partners* 3 (1): 160–168. https://doi.org/10.15173/ijsap.v3i1.3497

Irizarry, Jason G., and John Raible. 2014. "'A Hidden Part of Me': Latino/a Students, Silencing, and the Epidermalization of Inferiority." *Equity & Excellence in Education* 47 (4): 430–444. https://doi.org/10.1080/10665684.2014.958970

Iverson, Susan VanDeventer. 2007. "Camouflaging Power and Privilege: A Critical Race Analysis of University Diversity Policies." *Educational Administration Quarterly* 43 (5): 586–611.

Jack, Anthony A. 2019. *The Privileged Poor: How Elite Colleges Are Failing Disadvantaged Students.* Cambridge, MA: Harvard University Press.

James, Carl E. 2012. "Strategies of Engagement: How Racialized Faculty Negotiate the University System." *Canadian Ethnic Studies* 44 (2): 133–152.

Jensen, Kathrine Sophie Hornborg, and Dawn Bagnall. 2015. "Student Teaching and Learning Consultants: Developing Conversations About Teaching and Learning." *Journal of Educational Innovation, Partnership, and Change* 1 (1). https://journals.gre.ac.uk/index.php/studentchangeagents/issue/view/35

Jones-Devitt, Stella, Liz Austen, Elizabeth Chitwood, Alan Donnelly, Carolyn Fearn, Caroline Heaton, Gabrielle Latham, Jill LeBihan, Andrew Middleton, and Matthew Morgan. 2017. "Creation and Confidence: BME Students as Academic Partners . . . but Where Were the Staff?" *Journal of Educational Innovation Partnership and Change* 3 (1): 278–285.

Jonsson, Maya. Forthcoming. "Five Reasons Why Working as a Student Partner Is Energizing." *International Journal for Students as Partners.*

Joseph, Tiffany D., and Laura E. Hirshfield. 2011. "'Why Don't You Get Somebody New to Do It?' Race and Cultural Taxation in the Academy." *Ethnic and Racial Studies* 34 (1): 121–141. https://doi.org/10.1080/01419870.2010.496489

Kahn, Peter E. 2017. "The Flourishing and Dehumanization of Students in Higher Education." *Journal of Critical Realism* 16 (4): 368–382.

Kandiko Howson, Camille, and Saranne Weller. 2016. "Defining Pedagogic Expertise: Students and New Lecturers as Co-Developers in Learning and Teaching." *Teaching & Learning Inquiry* 4 (2). https://doi.org/10.20343/teachlearninqu.4.2.6

Kaur, Amrita, Rasna Awang-Hashim, and Manvender Kaur. 2018. "Students' Experiences of Co-Creating Classroom Instruction With Faculty: A Case Study in Eastern Context." *Teaching in Higher Education* 24 (4): 461–477. https://doi.org/10.1080/13562517.2018.1487930

Kaur, Amrita, and Toh Yong Bing. 2020. "Untangling the Power Dynamics in Forging Student-Faculty Collaboration." In *Building Courage, Confidence, and Capacity in Learning and Teaching Through Student-Faculty Partnership: Stories From Across Contexts and Arenas of Practice,* edited by Alison Cook-Sather and Chanelle Wilson, 61–70. Lanham, MD: Lexington Books.

Kehler, Angela, Roselynn Verwoord, and Heather Smith. 2017. "We Are the Process: Reflections on the Underestimation of Power in Students as Partners in Practice." *International Journal of Students as Partners* 1 (1). https://doi.org/10.15173/ijsap.v1i1.3176

Kendi, Ibram X. 2019. *How To Be an Antiracist.* New York, NY: One World.

Kezar, Adrianna, Trecia Bertram Gallant, and Jaime Lester. 2011. "Everyday People Making a Difference on College Campuses: The Tempered Grassroots Leadership Tactics of Faculty and Staff." *Studies in Higher Education* 36 (2): 129–151.

Kidd, Ian James, José Medina, and Gaile Pohlhaus Jr., Eds. 2017. *The Routledge Handbook of Epistemic Injustice.* Abingdon, UK: Routledge.

Koltun-Fromm, Kenneth, and Amaka Eze. 2019. "Dwelling in Discomfort." *Teaching and Learning Together in Higher Education* 28. https://repository.brynmawr.edu/tlthe/vol1/iss28/5/

Kotzee, Ben. 2017. "Education and Epistemic Injustice." In *The Routledge Handbook of Epistemic Injustice*, edited by Ian James Kidd, José Medina, and Gaile Pohlhaus Jr., 324–335. Abingdon, UK: Routledge.

Kupatadze, Ketevan. 2019. "Opportunities Presented by the Forced Occupation of Liminal Space. *International Journal for Students as Partners* 3 (1): 22–33. https://doi.org/10.15173/ijsap.v3i1.3744

Kwak, Naejin, S. Gabriela Gavrila, and Francisco O. Ramirez. 2019. "Enacting Diversity in American Higher Education." In *Universities as Agencies. Reputation and Professionalization*, edited by Tom Christensen, Åse Gornitzka, and Francisco O. Ramirez, 209–228. Cham, CH: Palgrave Macmillan.

Ladson-Billings, Gloria. 1995. "Toward a Theory of Culturally Relevant Pedagogy." *American Educational Research Journal* 32 (3): 465–491.

Le, Benjamin, and Maya Gorstein. 2019. "How I Learned to Embrace the Awkward Silences to Promote Class Participation." *Teaching and Learning Together in Higher Education* 28. https://repository.brynmawr.edu/cgi/viewcontent.cgi?article=1219&context=tlthe

Lenihan-Ikin, Isabella, Brad Olsen, Kathryn A. Sutherland, Emma Tennent, and Marc Wilson. 2020. "Partnership as a Civic Process." In *The Power of Partnership: Students, Faculty, and Staff Revolutionizing Higher Education,* edited by Lucy

Mercer-Mapstone and Sophia Abbot, 87–98. Elon, NC: Elon University Center for Engaged Learning. https://doi.org/10.36284/celelon.oa2

Leota, Ali, and Kathryn Sutherland. 2020. "'With Your Basket of Knowledge and My Basket of Knowledge, the People Will Prosper': Learning and Leading in a Student-Staff Partnership Program." In *Building Courage, Confidence, and Capacity in Learning and Teaching Through Student-Faculty Partnership: Stories From Across Contexts and Arenas of Practice,* edited by Alison Cook-Sather and Chanelle Wilson, 93–102. Lanham, MD: Lexington Books.

LePeau, Lucy A., Sarah Socorro Hurtado, and Latosha Williams. 2019. "Institutionalizing Diversity Agendas: Presidents' Councils for Diversity as Mechanisms for Strategic Change." *Journal of Student Affairs Research and Practice* 56 (2): 123–137.

Liebow, Nabina. 2016. "Internalized Oppression and Its Varied Moral Harms: Self Perceptions of Reduced Agency and Criminality." *Hypatia* 31 (4): 713–729. https://doi.org/10.1111/hypa.12265

Lillehaugen, Brook Danielle, and Eliza Cooney. 2019. "Seeing Homework Through Students' Eyes: From Pressured Performance to Intentional Learning." *Teaching and Learning Together in Higher Education* 28. https://repository.brynmawr.edu/cgi/viewcontent.cgi?article=1220&context=tlthe

Linder, Chris, Stephen John Quaye, Alex C. Lange, Ricky Ericka Roberts, Marvette C. Lacy, and Wilson Kwamogi Okello. 2019. "'A Student Should Have the Privilege of Just Being a Student': Student Activism as Labor." *The Review of Higher Education* 42 (5): 37–62.

Lo, Seung Wan (Winnie). 2016. "Towards a Nuanced Understanding of Inclusion and Exclusion: A Bourdieusian Interpretation of Chinese Students' Higher Education Experience in Canada." PhD diss., McMaster University.

Lorenzo, Adilene. 2020. "My Personal Troubled Transitions Into Student-Teacher Partnerships." *Teaching and Learning Together in Higher Education*, 30. https://repository.brynmawr.edu/tlthe/vol1/iss30/6/

Luker, Morgan, and Benjamin Morris. 2016. "Five Things I Learned From Working With the Student-Consultant for Teaching and Learning Program." *Teaching and Learning Together in Higher Education* 17. http://repository.brynmawr.edu/tlthe/vol1/iss17/2

MacDonald, Nancy, Wanda Bernard, Carolyn Campbell, Jeanne Fay, Judy MacDonald, and Brenda Richard. 2003. "Managing Institutional Practices to Promote and Strengthen Diversity: One School's Journey." In *Emerging Perspectives on Anti-Oppressive Practice*, edited by Wes Shera, 467–487. Toronto, ON: Canadian Scholars' Press.

Maldonado, David Emiliano Zapata, Robert Rhoads, and Tracy Lachica Buenavista. 2005. "The Student-Initiated Retention Project: Theoretical Contributions and the Role of Self-Empowerment." *American Educational Research Journal* 42 (4): 605–638.

Mann, Sarah J. 2001. "Alternative Perspectives on the Student Experience: Alienation and Engagement." *Studies in Higher Education* 26 (1): 7–19.

Marquis, Elizabeth. 2018. "Embracing and/or Avoiding the Risks of Partnership: A Faculty Perspective." *Teaching and Learning Together in Higher Education* 24. https://repository.brynmawr.edu/tlthe/vol1/iss24/9/

Marquis, Elizabeth. 2019. "Engaging as Partners: Student-Faculty Partnership and the Promise of More Equitable Institutions." Presentation at the 2019 Symposium on Scholarship of Teaching and Learning, Banff, AB, November 7–9.

Marquis, Elizabeth, Christine Black, and Mick Healey. 2017. "Responding to the Challenges of Student-Staff Partnership: Reflections of Participants at an International Summer Institute." *Teaching in Higher Education* 22 (6): 720–735.

Marquis, Elizabeth, Emily Carrasco-Acosta, Alise de Bie, Srikripa Krishna Prasad, Sneha Wadhwani, and Cherie Woolmer. 2019. "Pedagogical Partnerships and Equity in the Classroom: Insights From One Partnership Program." Presentation at the 2019 Symposium on Scholarship of Teaching and Learning, Banff, AB, November 7–9.

Marquis, Elizabeth, Alise de Bie, Alison Cook-Sather, Srikripa Krishna Prasad, Leslie Luqueño, and Anita Ntem. Forthcoming. "'I Saw a Change': Enhancing Classroom Equity Through Student-Faculty Pedagogical Partnership." *Canadian Journal for the Scholarship of Teaching and Learning.*

Marquis, Elizabeth, Ann Fudge Schormans, Bonny Jung, Christina Vietinghoff, Rob Wilton, and Sue Baptiste. 2016. "Charting the Landscape of Accessible Education for Post-Secondary Students With Disabilities." *Canadian Journal for Disability Studies* 5 (2): 41–71. https://doi.org/10.15353/cjds.v5i2.272

Marquis, Elizabeth, Rachel Guitman, Christine Black, Mick Healey, Kelly E. Matthews, and Lucie Sam Dvorakova. 2019. "Growing Partnership Communities: What Experiences of an International Institute Suggest About Developing Student-Staff Partnership in Higher Education." *Innovations in Education and Teaching International* 56 (2): 184–194. https://doi.org/10.1080/14703297.20 18.1424012

Marquis, Elizabeth, Rachel Guitman, Elaina Nguyen, and Cherie Woolmer. 2020. "'It's a Little Complicated for Me: Faculty Social Location and Experiences of Pedagogical Partnership." *Higher Education Research and Development.* https://doi.org/10.1080/07294360.2020.1806789

Marquis, Elizabeth, Zeeshan Haqqee, Sabrina Kirby, Alexandra Liu, Varun Puri, Robert Cockcroft, Lori Goff, and Kris Knorr. 2017. "Connecting Students and Staff for Teaching and Learning Inquiry: The McMaster Student Partners Program." In *Disciplinary Approaches to Connecting the Higher Education Curriculum,* edited by Brent Carnell and Dilly Fung, 203–216. London, UK: University College of London Press.

Marquis, Elizabeth, Ajitha Jayaratnam, Tianqi Lei, and Anamika Mishra. 2019. "Motivators, Barriers, and Understandings: How Students at Four Universities Perceive Student-Faculty Partnership Programs." *Higher Education Research and Development* 38 (6): 1240–1254. https://doi.org/10.1080/07294360.2019.1638349

Marquis, Elizabeth, Ajitha Jayaratnam, Anamika Mishra, and Ksenia Rybkina. 2018. "'I Feel Like Some Students Are Better Connected': Students' Perspectives on

Applying for Extracurricular Partnership Opportunities." *International Journal for Students as Partners* 2 (1): 64–81. https://doi.org/10.15173/ijsap.v2i1.3300

Marquis, Elizabeth, Bonny Jung, Ann Fudge Schormans, Sara Lukmanji, Robert Wilton, and Sue Baptiste. 2016. "Developing Inclusive Educators: Enhancing the Accessibility of Teaching and Learning in Higher Education." *International Journal for Academic Development* 21 (4): 337–349.

Marquis, Elizabeth, Bonny Jung, Ann Fudge Schormans, Susan Vajoczki, Robert Wilton, Susan Baptiste, and Anju Joshi. 2012. "Creating, Resisting or Neglecting Change: Exploring the Complexities of Accessible Education for Students With Disabilities." *Canadian Journal for the Scholarship of Teaching & Learning* 3 (2). http://ir.lib.uwo.ca/cjsotl_rcacea/vol3/iss2/

Marquis, Elizabeth, Emily Power, and Melanie Yin. 2019. "Promoting and/or Evading Change: The Role of Student-Staff Partnerships in Staff Teaching Development." *Journal of Further and Higher Education* 43 (10): 1315–1330. https://doi.org/10.1080/0309877X.2018.1483013

Marquis, Elizabeth, Varun Puri, Stephanie Wan, Arshad Ahmad, Lori Goff, Kris Knorr, Ianitza Vassileva, and Jason Woo. 2016. "Navigating the Threshold of Student-Staff Partnerships: A Case Study From an Ontario Teaching and Learning Institute." *International Journal for Academic Development* 21 (1): 4–15.

Marquis, Elizabeth, Alan Santinele Martino, and Tianna Follwell. 2020. "Enacting and/or Contesting the 'Normal TA Body': Social Location and the Experiences of Teaching Assistants." Unpublished manuscript.

Marquis, Elizabeth, Cherie Woolmer, Rachel Guitman, and Elaina Nguyen. 2019. "Academic Staff Perspectives on Student-Faculty Partnerships: Redressing or Reinforcing Inequity in Higher Education?" In *3rd EuroSOTL Conference Proceedings* (Bilbao, Basque Country: Universidad del Pais Vasco), 588–595. https://www.ehu.eus/documents/8301386/10560621/Actas-EuroSoTL-Conference-2019.pdf/1a7d5867-e222-4aab-6f92-a7948f1fbd67

Martin, Jonathan. 2008. "Pedagogy of the Alienated: Can Freirian Teaching Reach Working-Class Students?" *Equity & Excellence in Education* 41 (1): 31–44. https://doi.org/10.1080/10665680701773776

Martínez, Melissa A., Aurora Chang, and Anjalé D. Welton. 2017. "Assistant Professors of Color Confront the Inequitable Terrain of Academia: A Community Cultural Wealth Perspective." *Race, Ethnicity and Education* 20 (5): 696–710. https://doi.org/10.1080/13613324.2016.1150826

Masta, Stephanie. 2018. "'I Am Exhausted': Everyday Occurrences of Being Native American." *International Journal of Qualitative Studies in Education* 31 (9): 821–835. https://doi.org/10.1080/09518398.2018.1499984

Mathrani, Sasha. 2018. "Building Relationships, Navigating Discomfort and Uncertainty, and Translating My Voice in New Contexts." *Teaching and Learning Together in Higher Education* 23. https://repository.brynmawr.edu/tlthe/vol1/iss23/6

Matthews, Kelly E. 2017. "Five Propositions for Genuine Students as Partners Practice." *International Journal for Students as Partners* 1 (2). https://doi.org/10.15173/ijsap.v1i2.3315

Matthews, Kelly E., Alison Cook-Sather, Anita Acai, Sam Lucie Dvorakova, Peter Felten, Elizabeth Marquis, and Lucy Mercer-Mapstone. 2019. "Toward Theories of Partnership Praxis: An Analysis of Interpretive Framing in Literature on Students as Partners in Teaching and Learning." *Higher Education Research & Development* 38 (2): 280–293. https://doi.org/10.1080/07294360.2018.1530199

Matthews, Kelly E., Alison Cook-Sather, and Mick Healey. 2018. "Connecting Learning, Teaching, and Research through Student-Staff Partnerships: Toward Universities as Egalitarian Learning Communities." In *Shaping Higher Education with Students: Ways to Connect Research and Teaching*, edited by Vincent C. H. Tong, Alex Standen, and Mina Sotiriou, 23–29. London, UK: University College of London Press.

Matthews, Kelly E., Alexander Dwyer, Stuart Russell, and Eimear Enright. 2019. "It Is a Complicated Thing: Leaders' Conceptions of Students as Partners in the Neoliberal University." *Studies in Higher Education* 44 (12): 2196–2207. https://doi.org/10.1080/03075079.2018.1482268

Matthews, Kelly E., Lucy Mercer-Mapstone, Sam Lucie Dvorakova, Anita Acai, Alison Cook-Sather, Peter Felten, Mick Healey, Ruth L. Healey, and Elizabeth Marquis. 2019. "Enhancing Outcomes and Reducing Inhibitors to the Engagement of Students and Staff in Learning and Teaching Partnerships: Implications for Academic Development." *International Journal for Academic Development* 24 (3): 246–259. https://doi.org/10.1080/1360144X.2018.1545233

May, Vivian M. 2014. "'Speaking Into the Void'? Intersectionality Critiques and Epistemic Backlash." *Hypatia* 29 (1): 94–112. https://doi.org/10.1111/hypa.12060

Mayuzumi, Kimine. 2015. "Navigating Orientalism: Asian Women Faculty in the Canadian Academy." *Race Ethnicity and Education* 18 (2): 277–296.

McDonald, Jeremy, and Lori Ward. 2017. "Why So Many Canadian Universities Know So Little About Their Own Racial Diversity." *CBC News,* March 21, 2017. https://www.cbc.ca/news/canada/race-canadian-universities-1.4030537

McIntosh, Peggy. 1990. "White Privilege: Unpacking the Invisible Knapsack." *Independent School* 49 (2): 31–36. https://ocufa.on.ca/assets/White_Privilege.pdf

McMaster University. 2019. "Toward Inclusive Excellence: McMaster University's Equity, Diversity and Inclusion (EDI) Strategy." https://equity.mcmaster.ca/app/uploads/2020/07/EDI-Strategy-Towards-Inclusive-Excellence-2020.pdf

McMaster University. n.d. "McMaster Fast Facts." https://www.mcmaster.ca/opr/html/opr/fast_facts/main/about.html

McNair, Tia Brown, Estela Mara Bensimon, and Lindsey Malcolm-Piqueux. 2020. *From Equity Talk to Equity Walk: Expanding Practitioner Knowledge for Racial Justice in Higher Education.* San Francisco, CA: Jossey-Bass.

Mercer-Mapstone, Lucy. 2019. "Student-Staff Partnership as Collective Curricular Activism in Curriculum Liberation Efforts." *Center for Engaged Learning Blog,* January 29, 2019. https://www.centerforengagedlearning.org/student-staff-partnership-as-collective-curricular-activism/

Mercer-Mapstone, Lucy. 2020. "The Student–Staff Partnership Movement: Striving for Inclusion as We Push Sectorial Change." *International Journal for Academic Development* 25 (2): 121–133. https://doi.org/10.1080/1360144X.2019.1631171

Mercer-Mapstone, Lucy, and Catherine Bovill. 2020. "Equity and Diversity in Institutional Approaches to Student–Staff Partnership Schemes in Higher Education." *Studies in Higher Education*. https://doi.org/10.1080/03075079.2019.1620721

Mercer-Mapstone, Lucy, Lucie Sam Dvorakova, Lauren J. Groenendijk, and Kelly E. Matthews. 2017. "Idealism, Conflict, Leadership, and Labels: Reflections on Co-Facilitation as Partnership Practice." *Teaching and Learning Together in Higher Education* 21. https://repository.brynmawr.edu/cgi/viewcontent.cgi?article=1170&context=tlthe

Mercer-Mapstone, Lucy, Sam Lucie Dvorakova, Kelly E. Matthews, Sophia Abbot, Breagh Cheng, Peter Felten, Kris Knorr, Elizabeth Marquis, Rafaella Shammas, and Kelly Swaim. 2017. "A Systematic Literature Review of Students as Partners in Higher Education." *International Journal for Students as Partners* 1 (1). https://doi.org/10.15173/ijsap.v1i1.3119

Mercer-Mapstone, Lucy, Rachel Guitman, and Anita Acai. 2019. "Reflecting Gendered Experiences of Student-Staff Partnership: A Student Standpoint Using Poetic Transcription." *Teaching in Higher Education* 24 (6): 809–818. https://doi.org/10.1080/13562517.2019.1602761

Mercer-Mapstone, Lucy, Maisha Islam, and Tamara Reid. 2021. "Are We Just Engaging 'The Usual Suspects'? Challenges In and Practical Strategies for Supporting Equity and Diversity in Student–Staff Partnership Initiatives." *Teaching in Higher Education* 26 (2): 227–245. https://doi.org/10.1080/13562517.2019.1655396

Mercer-Mapstone, Lucy, and Gina Mercer. 2018. "A Dialogue Between Partnership and Feminism: Deconstructing Power and Exclusion in Higher Education." *Teaching in Higher Education* 23 (1): 137–143. https://doi.org/10.1080/135625 17.2017.1391198

Michell, Adrianna. 2019. "Spotlight On: Teaching at the Intersections." *International Institute on Students as Partners Connect* (blog), July 24, 2019. https://macblog.mcmaster.ca/summer-institute/2019/07/24/spotlight-on-teaching-at-the-intersections/

Mihans, Richard, Deborah Long, and Peter Felten. 2008. "Power and Expertise: Student-Faculty Collaboration in Course Design and the Scholarship of Teaching and Learning." *International Journal for the Scholarship of Teaching & Learning* 2 (2). http://digitalcommons.georgiasouthern.edu/ij-sotl/vol2/iss2/16/

Miller, Ryan A. 2015. "'Sometimes You Feel Invisible': Performing Queer/Disabled in the University Classroom." *The Educational Forum* 79 (4): 377–393.

Moore-Cherry, Niamh, Ruth Healey, Dawn T. Nicholson, and Will Andrews. 2016. "Inclusive Partnership: Enhancing Student Engagement in Geography." *Journal of Geography in Higher Education* 40 (1): 84–103. https://doi.org/10.1080/0309 8265.2015.1066316

Moriarty, Jo, and Jo Murray. 2007. "Who Wants to Be a Social Worker? Using Routine Published Data to Identify Trends in the Numbers of People Applying for and Completing Social Work Programmes in England." *British Journal of Social Work* 37 (4): 715–733. https://doi.org/10.1093/bjsw/bch325

Moys, Jeanne-Louise. 2018. "Promoting Diversity Through Developing a Sense of Community." *International Journal for Students as Partners* 2 (2): 135–143. https://doi.org/10.15173/ijsap.v2i2.3547

Narayanan, Desika, and Sophia Abbot. 2020. "Increasing the Participation of Underrepresented Minorities in STEM Classes Through Student-Instructor Partnerships." In *The Power of Partnership: Students, Faculty, and Staff Revolutionizing Higher Education,* edited by Lucy Mercer-Mapstone and Sophia Abbot, 181–195. Elon, NC: Elon University Center for Engaged Learning. https://doi.org/10.36284/celelon.oa2

Narkiss, Doron, and Iska Naaman. 2020. "Voicing and Reflecting in a Pedagogical Partnership." In *Building Courage, Confidence, and Capacity in Learning and Teaching Through Student-Faculty Partnership: Stories From Across Contexts and Arenas of Practice,* edited by Alison Cook-Sather and Chanelle Wilson, 39–48. Lanham, MD: Lexington Books.

Nave, Lillian, Alejandra Aguilar, Matthew Barnes, Aliesha Knauer, Erica-Grace Lubamba, Kendall Miller, Verolinka Slawson, and Taylor Taylor. 2018. "On Confederate Monuments, Racial Strife, and the Politics of Power on a Southern Campus." *Teaching and Learning Together in Higher Education* 24. https://repository.brynmawr.edu/tlthe/vol1/iss24/3

Neary, Mike. 2010. "Student as Producer: A Pedagogy for the Avant-Garde?" *Learning Exchange* 1 (1). https://cpb-eu-w2.wpmucdn.com/blogs.lincoln.ac.uk/dist/e/185/files/2014/03/15-72-1-pb-1.pdf

Neary, Mike. 2016. "Student as Producer: The Struggle for the Idea of the University." *Other Education: The Journal of Educational Alternatives* 5 (1): 89–94. https://www.othereducation.org/index.php/OE/article/view/163

Neary, Mike, and Gary Saunders. 2016. "Student as Producer and the Politics of Abolition: Making a New Form of Dissident Institution?" *Critical Education* 7 (5). http://ojs.library.ubc.ca/index.php/criticaled/article/view/18600

Ntem, Anita. 2017. "Relating Resistance and Resilience in Student-Faculty Pedagogical Partnership." Poster presentation, McMaster Summer Institute on Students as Partners, Hamilton, ON, May.

Ntem, Anita. 2020. "Personal Growth Through Traditional and Radical Partnerships." In *The Power of Partnership: Students, Staff, and Faculty Revolutionizing Higher Education,* edited by Lucy Mercer-Mapstone and Sophia Abbot, 197–204. Elon, NC: Elon University Center for Engaged Learning. https://doi.org/10.36284/celelon.oa2

Ntem, Anita, and Alison Cook-Sather. 2018. "Resistances and Resiliencies in Pedagogical Partnership: Student Partners' Perspectives." *International Journal for Students as Partners* 2 (1): 82–96. https://doi.org/10.15173/ijsap.v2i1.3372

Office of Community Engagement, McMaster University. 2018. "Community-Engaged Education Toolkit." https://community.mcmaster.ca/education/community-engaged-education-toolkit/

Ortquist-Ahrens, Leslie, Anne Bruder, Khadijah Seay, and Mia Rybeck. 2021. "Building Partnership Through Partnership: The Power of a Post-Bac Fellow Position in Developing Student-Faculty Partnership Programs." Unpublished manuscript.

O'Shea, Sarah. 2018. "Equity and Students as Partners: The Importance of Inclusive Relationships." *International Journal for Students as Partners* 2 (2): 16–20. https://doi.org/10.15173/ijsap.v2i2.3628

Padden, Lisa, and Carol Ellis. 2015. "Disability Awareness and University Staff Training in Ireland." *Journal of Postsecondary Education and Disability* 28 (4): 433–435. https://eric.ed.gov/?id=EJ1093559

Pallant, Miriam. 2014. "The Dynamics of Expertise." *Teaching and Learning Together in Higher Education* 11. http://repository.brynmawr.edu/tlthe/vol1/iss11/2

Paris, Django. 2012. "Culturally Sustaining Pedagogy: A Needed Change in Stance, Terminology, and Practice." *Educational Researcher* 41 (3): 93–97. https://doi.org/10.3102/0013189X12441244

Patton, Lori D., and Stephanie Bondi. 2015. "Nice White Men or Social Justice Allies?: Using Critical Race Theory to Examine How White Male Faculty and Administrators Engage in Ally Work." *Race, Ethnicity and Education* 18 (4): 488–514. https://doi.org/10.1080/13613324.2014.1000289

Patton, Lori D., Berenice Sánchez, Jacqueline Mac, and D. L. Stewart. 2019. "An Inconvenient Truth About 'Progress': An Analysis of the Promises and Perils of Research on Campus Diversity Initiatives." *The Review of Higher Education* 42 (5): 173–198. https://doi.org/10.1353/rhe.2019.0049

Perez, Kerstin. 2016. "Striving Toward a Space for Equity and Inclusion in Physics Classrooms." *Teaching and Learning Together in Higher Education* 18. http://repository.brynmawr.edu/tlthe/vol1/iss18/3

Perez-Putnam, Miriam. 2016. "Belonging and Brave Space as Hope for Personal and Institutional Inclusion." *Teaching and Learning Together in Higher Education* 18. http://repository.brynmawr.edu/tlthe/vol1/iss18/2

Pittman, Chavella T. 2010. "Race and Gender Oppression in the Classroom: The Experiences of Women Faculty of Color With White Male Students." *Teaching Sociology* 38 (3): 183–196. https://doi.org/10.1177/0092055X10370120

Pizarro, Marc. 1998. "Contesting Dehumanization: Chicana/o Spiritualization, Revolutionary Possibility, and the Curriculum." *Aztlan: A Journal of Chicano Studies* 23 (1): 55–76. https://doi.org/10.1207/s1532771xjle0303_2

Pohlhaus, Gaile, Jr. 2017. "Varieties of Epistemic Injustice." In *The Routledge Handbook of Epistemic Injustice,* edited by Ian James Kidd, José Medina, and Gaile Pohlhaus Jr., 13–26. Abingdon: Routledge.

Poolokasingham, Gauthamie, Lisa B. Spanierman, Sela Kleiman, and Sara Houshmand. 2014. "'Fresh Off the Boat?' Racial Microaggressions That Target South Asian Canadian Students." *Journal of Diversity in Higher Education* 7 (3): 194–210. https://doi.org/10.1037/a0037285

Pounder, James S., Elizabeth Ho Hung-lam, and Julie May Groves. 2016. "Faculty-Student Engagement in Teaching Observation and Assessment: A Hong Kong Initiative." *Assessment & Evaluation in Higher Education* 41 (8): 1193–1205. https://doi.org/10.1080/02602938.2015.1071779

Queen's University. 2019. "Education (Training)." https://www.queensu.ca/hreo/onedi

Ramsden, Paul. 2008. "The Future of Higher Education Teaching and the Student Experience." London, UK: BIS. https://www.advance-he.ac.uk/knowledge-hub/future-higher-education-teaching-and-student-experience

Reckson, Lindsay V. 2014. "The Weather in Hemingway." *Teaching and Learning Together in Higher Education* 11. http://repository.brynmawr.edu/tlthe/vol1/iss11/6

Reeve, Donna. 2012. "Psycho-Emotional Disablism: The Missing Link?" In *The Routledge Handbook of Disability Studies,* edited by Nick Watson, Alana Roulstone, and Carol Thomas, 78–92. London, UK: Routledge.

Reyes, Reynaldo, and Emiliano Villarreal. 2016. "Wanting the Unwanted Again: Safeguarding Against Normalizing Dehumanization and Discardability of Marginalized, 'Unruly' English-Learning Latinos in Our Schools." *The Urban Review* 48 (4): 543–559. https://doi.org/10.1007/s11256-016-0367-8

Reyes, Victoria, and Kirsten Adams. 2017. "Navigating a Difficult Journey: Reflections on How a Student-Faculty Partnership Helped Address Racial Tensions in a Social Science Course." *International Journal for Students as Partners* 1 (2). https://doi.org/10.15173/ijsap.v1i2.3262

Rhoads, Robert A., Tracy Lachica Buenavista, and David E. Z. Maldonado. 2004. "Students of Color Helping Others Stay in College: A Grassroots Effort." *About Campus* 9 (3): 10–17.

Ropers-Huilman, Becky, Laura Carwile, and Kathy Barnett. 2005. "Student Activists' Characterizations of Administrators in Higher Education: Perceptions of Power in 'the System.'" *The Review of Higher Education* 28 (3): 295–312.

Sayles, Michelle, with Alise de Bie. 2018. "Open ACCESSibility: An Illustrated Story of Disability Advocacy @ McMaster." https://macblog.mcmaster.ca/flexforwardresource/2019/02/04/open-accessibility-an-illustrated-story-of-disability-advocacy/

Schlosser, Joel, and Abigail Sweeney. 2015. "One Year of Collaboration: Reflections on Student-Faculty Partnership." *Teaching and Learning Together in Higher Education* 15. https://repository.brynmawr.edu/tlthe/vol1/iss15/2/

Seale, Jane, Suanne Gibson, Joanna Haynes, and Alice Potter. 2015. "Power and Resistance: Reflections on the Rhetoric and Reality of Using Participatory Methods to Promote Student Voice and Engagement in Higher Education." *Journal of Further and Higher Education* 39 (4): 534–552.

Seow, Yvette. 2019. "Taking a Small Step Toward Partnership." *Teaching and Learning Together in Higher Education* 27. https://repository.brynmawr.edu/tlthe/vol1/iss27/5/

Sharp-Hoskins, Kellie, and Amy E. Robillard. 2012. "Narrating the 'Good Teacher' in Rhetoric and Composition: Ideology, Affect, Complicity." *JAC: A Journal of Composition Theory* 32: 305–336.

Shittu, Rasaaq. 2020. "As a Black Student at Haverford College, I Know What Racism Looks Like at 'Liberal' Institutions." *Philadelphia Inquirer,* July 15, 2020. https://www.inquirer.com/opinion/commentary/university-college-diversity-haverford-black-lives-matter-20200715.html

Sible, Jill, Jeremy Wojdak, Laura Gough, Patrice Moss, and Nadjla Miranda Mouchrek. 2019. "Sustaining Institutional Change for Inclusive Excellence." Presentation at the Thematic Symposium at the ASCN Transforming Institutions Conference. Pittsburgh, PA, April 3–5.

Sim, Jonathan Y. H. 2019. "The 'Face' Barriers to Partnership." *Teaching and Learning Together in Higher Education* 27. https://repository.brynmawr.edu/tlthe/vol1/iss27/4/

Simmons, Jack, Russell Lowery-Hart, Shawn T. Wahl, and Chad McBride. 2013. "Understanding the African-American Student Experience in Higher Education Through a Relational Dialectics Perspective." *Communication Education* 62 (4): 376–394.

Singh, Manroocha. 2018. "Moving from 'Us vs. Them' to 'Us' Through Working in Pedagogical Partnership." *Teaching and Learning Together in Higher Education* 23. https://repository.brynmawr.edu/tlthe/vol1/iss23/5/

Slater, Lisa. 2019. "Good White People: Settler Colonial Anxiety and the Endurance of Racism." *Emotions: History, Culture, Society* 3 (2): 266–281. https://doi.org/10.1163/2208522X-02010060

Smit, Renee. 2012. "Towards a Clearer Understanding of Student Disadvantage in Higher Education: Problematising Deficit Thinking." *Higher Education Research & Development* 31 (3): 369–380. https://doi.org/10.1080/07294360.2011.634383

Smith, Melissa. J. 2015. "It's a Balancing Act: The *Good* Teacher and *Ally* Identity." *Educational Studies* 51 (3): 223–243. https://doi.org/10.1080/00131946.2015.1033517

Smith, William A., Jalil Bishop Mustaffa, Chantal M. Jones, Tommy J. Curry, and Walter R. Allen. 2016. "'You Make Me Wanna Holler and Throw Up Both My Hands!': Campus Culture, Black Misandric Microaggressions, and Racial Battle Fatigue." *International Journal of Qualitative Studies in Education* 29 (9): 1189–1209. https://doi.org/10.1080/09518398.2016.1214296

Solorzano, Daniel, Miguel Ceja, and Tara Yosso. 2000. "Critical Race Theory, Racial Microaggressions, and Campus Racial Climate: The Experiences of African American College Students." *Journal of Negro Education* 29 (1/2): 60–73. https://www.jstor.org/stable/2696265

Spivak, Gayatri Chakravorty. 1988. "Can the Subaltern Speak?" In *Marxism and the Interpretation of Culture,* edited by Cary Nelson and Lawrence Grossberg, 271–313. Basingstoke, UK: Macmillan.

Stanway, Bonnie Rose, Yiyuan Cao, Tony Cannell, and Yihui Gu. 2019. "Tensions and Rewards: Behind the Scenes in a Cross-Cultural Student–Staff Partnership." *Journal of Studies in International Education* 23 (1): 30–48. https://doi.org/10.1177/1028315318813199

Stauffer, Jill. 2015. *Ethical Loneliness: The Injustice of Not Being Heard.* New York, NY: Columbia University Press.

Stewart, Dafina-Lazarus. 2017. "Language of Appeasement." *Inside Higher Ed,* March 30, 2017. https://www.insidehighered.com/views/2017/03/30/colleges-need-language-shift-not-one-you-think-essay

Strayhorn, Terrell L. 2012. *College Students' Sense of Belonging: A Key to Educational Success for All Students.* New York, NY: Routledge.

Suárez-Orozco, Carola, Saskias Casanova, Margary Martin, Dalal Katsiaficas, Veronica Cuellar, Naila Antonia Smith, and Sandra Isabel Dias. 2015. "Toxic Rain in Class: Classroom Interpersonal Microaggressions." *Educational Researcher* 44 (3): 151–160. https://doi.org/10.3102/0013189X15580314

Sullivan, Shannon. 2014. *Good White People: The Problem With Middle-Class White Anti-Racism.* New York, NY: SUNY Press.

Tamtik, Merli, and Melissa Guenter. 2019. "Policy Analysis of Equity, Diversity and Inclusion Strategies in Canadian Universities—How Far Have We Come?" *Canadian Journal of Higher Education* 49 (3): 41–56. https://doi.org/10.7202/1066634ar

Tatum, Beverly Daniel. 2015. "Can We Talk About Race? A Conversation With Beverly Daniel Tatum." Keynote address at the Professional and Organizational Development Network Conference, San Francisco, November 4–8. *I was there*

Thomas, Carol. 1999. *Female Forms: Experiencing and Understanding Disability.* Buckingham: McGraw-Hill Education.

Thomas, Carol. 2007. *Sociologies of Disability and Illness: Contested Ideas in Disability Studies and Medical Sociology.* London, UK: Macmillan International Higher Education.

Thomas, Liz. 2002. "Student Retention in Higher Education: The Role of Institutional Habitus." *Journal of Education Policy* 17 (4): 423–442. https://doi.org/10.1080/02680930210140257

Trow, Martin. 2007. "Reflections on the Transition from Elite to Mass to Universal Access: Forms and Phases of Higher Education in Modern Societies Since WWII." In *International Handbook of Higher Education*, edited by James F. Forest and Philip G. Altbach, 243–280. Dordrecht, NL: Springer.

Truth and Reconciliation Commission of Canada. 2012. "Truth and Reconciliation Commission of Canada: Calls to Action." http://trc.ca/assets/pdf/Calls_to_Action_English2.pdf

Tuitt, Frank. 2003. "Afterword: Realizing a More Inclusive Pedagogy." In *Race and Higher Education: Rethinking Pedagogy in Diverse College Classrooms,* edited by Annie Howell and Frank Tuitt, 243–268. Cambridge, MA: Harvard Educational Review.

Universities Canada. 2017. "Universities Canada Principles on Equity, Diversity, and Inclusion." https://www.univcan.ca/media-room/media-releases/universities-canada-principles-equity-diversity-inclusion/

Universities Canada. n.d. "Equity, Diversity and Inclusion Initiatives at Canadian Universities." https://www.univcan.ca/priorities/equity-diversity-inclusion/edi-stories/

Vaccaro, Annemarie, and Jasmine A. Mena. 2011. "It's Not Burnout, *It's More*: Queer College Activists of Color and Mental Health." *Journal of Gay & Lesbian Mental Health* 15 (4): 339–367. https://doi.org/10.1080/19359705.2011.600656

Van Dam, Lianne. 2016. Student Response to "Students as Partners: Reflections on a Conceptual Model." *Teaching and Learning Inquiry* 4 (2): 12–13. https://doi.org/10.20343/teachlearninqu.4.2.3

Vermette, D'Arcy. 2012. "Inclusion Is Killing Us." *Teaching Perspectives* 17: 18–19. https://moodle.stu.ca/pluginfile.php?file=/6082/mod_page/content/4/Teaching_Perspectives/Issue_17_-_TP_Fall_2012.pdf

Verwoord, Roselynn, and Heather Smith. 2020. "The P.O.W.E.R. Framework. Power Dimensions Shaping Students as Partners Processes." In *The Power of Partnership: Students, Faculty, and Staff Revolutionizing Higher Education*, edited by Lucy Mercer-Mapstone and Sophia Abbot, 29–42. Elon, NC: Elon University Center for Engaged Learning. https://doi.org/10.36284/celelon.oa2

Wallin, Patric, and Liselott Aarsand. 2019. "Challenging Spaces: Liminal Positions and Knowledge Relations in Dynamic Research Partnerships." *International Journal for Students as Partners* 3 (1): 69–83. https://doi.org/10.15173/ijsap.v3i1.3739

Walton, Gregory M., and Shannon T. Brady. 2017. "The Many Questions of Belonging." In *Handbook of Confidence and Motivation: Theory and Application*, edited by Andrew J. Elliot, Carol S. Dweck, and David S. Yeager, 272–293. New York, NY: The Guilford Press.

Walton, Gregory M., and Geoffrey L. Cohen. 2007. "A Question of Belonging: Race, Social Fit, and Achievement." *Journal of Personality and Social Psychology* 92 (1): 82–96. https://doi.org/10.1037/0022-3514.92.1.82

Wang, Yi, and Yonglin Jiang. 2012. "An Equal Partnership: Preparing for Faculty-Student Team Teaching of 'Cultural History of Chinese Astronomy.'" *Teaching and Learning Together in Higher Education* 6. https://repository.brynmawr.edu/tlthe/vol1/iss6/9/

Waqar, Yasira, and Abdul Moeed Asad. 2020. "Student as Co-Designer: Processes of Planning and Teaching With the Student in Mind." In *Building Courage, Confidence, and Capacity in Learning and Teaching Through Student-Faculty Partnership: Stories From Across Contexts and Arenas of Practice*, edited by Alison Cook-Sather and Chanelle Wilson, 71–79. Lanham, MD: Lexington Books.

Waterfield, Bea, Brenda B. Beagan, and Merlinda Weinberg. 2018. "Disabled Academics: A Case Study in Canadian Universities." *Disability & Society* 33 (3): 327–348. https://doi.org/10.1080/09687599.2017.1411251

Watermeyer, Brian Paul. 2009. "Conceptualising Psycho-Emotional Aspects of Disablist Discrimination and Impairment: Towards a Psychoanalytically Informed Disability Studies." PhD diss., University of Stellenbosch.

White, Helen, and Paul Wynkoop. 2019. "Pink Bagels and Persistence." *Teaching and Learning Together in Higher Education* 28. https://repository.brynmawr.edu/tlthe/vol1/iss28/6/

Whynacht, Ardath. 2017. "Prison in the Spaces Between Us: Abolition, Austerity, and the Possibility of Compassionate Containment." In *What Moves Us: The Lives and Times of the Radical Imagination*, edited by Alex Khasnabish and Max Haiven, 57–68. Toronto, ON: Fernwood Press & Upping the Anti.

Williams, Damon A., Joseph B. Berger, and Shederick A. McClendon. 2005. *Toward a Model of Inclusive Excellence and Change in Postsecondary Institutions*. Washington DC: Association for American Colleges & Universities.

Willimon, William H., and Thomas H. Naylor. 1995. *The Abandoned Generation: Rethinking Higher Education.* Grand Rapids, MI: Wm. B. Eerdmans Publishing.

Wilson, Erin K. 2017. "'Power Differences' and 'the Power of Difference': The Dominance of Secularism as Ontological Injustice." *Globalizations* 14 (7): 1076–1093. https://doi.org/10.1080/14747731.2017.1308062

Wilson, Sean, Julie Phillips, Helen Meskhidze, Claire Lockard, Peter Felten, Susannah McGowan, and Stephen Bloch-Schulman. 2020. "From Novelty to Norm: Moving Beyond Exclusion and the Double Justification Problem in Student-Faculty Partnerships." In *The Power of Partnership: Students, Faculty, and Staff Revolutionizing Higher Education,* edited by Lucy Mercer-Mapstone and Sophia Abbot, 43–60. Elon, NC: Elon University Center for Engaged Learning. https://doi.org/10.36284/celelon.oa2

Wing Sue, Derald, Ed. 2010. *Microaggressions and Marginality: Manifestation, Dynamics, and Impact.* Hoboken, NJ: Wiley.

Woolmer, Cherie. 2018. "The Battleground for Students as Partners: Applying the Habermasian Concept of Colonisation to Explore the Appropriation of Practice." *Student Engagement in Higher Education Journal* 2 (1): 120–123. https://sehej.raise-network.com/raise/article/view/Bryson

Woolmer, Cherie, Cathy Bovill, Alise de Bie, and Elizabeth Marquis. 2019. "Navigating Ethical Tensions in Student-Faculty Partnerships." Panel at the ISSOTL Conference, Atlanta, GA, October 9–12.

Woolmer, Cherie, Elizabeth Marquis, Erin Aspenlieder, and Lori Goff. 2019. "Student-Staff Partnerships in Teaching and Learning." In *A Handbook for Teaching and Learning in Higher Education,* 5th ed., edited by Stephanie Marshall, 81–94. London, UK: Routledge.

Yahlnaaw. 2019. "T'aats'iigang—Stuffing a Jar Full." *International Journal for Students as Partners* 3 (2): 6–10. https://doi.org/10.15173/ijsap.v3i2.4081

Yeager, David S., Gregory M. Walton, Shannon T. Brady, Ezgi N. Akcinar, David Paunesku, Laura Keane, Donald Kamentz, Gretchen Ritter, Angela Lee Duckworth, Robert Urstein, Eric M. Gomez, Hazel Rose Markus, Geoffrey L. Cohen, and Carol S. Dweck. 2016. "Teaching a Lay Theory Before College Narrows Achievement Gaps at Scale." *Proceedings of the National Academy of Sciences of the United States of America* 113 (24): E3341–E3348.

Yosso, Tara, William Smith, Miguel Ceja, and Daniel Solórzano. 2009. "Critical Race Theory, Racial Microaggressions, and Campus Racial Climate for Latina/o Undergraduates." *Harvard Educational Review* 79 (4): 659–691. https://doi.org/10.17763/haer.79.4.m6867014157m707l

Zembylas, Michalinos. 2017. "Practicing an Ethic of Discomfort as an Ethic of Care in Higher Education Teaching." *Critical Studies in Teaching and Learning* 5 (1): 1–17. https://www.ajol.info/index.php/cristal/article/view/158623

**Alise de Bie** is a postdoctoral research fellow in the Paul R. MacPherson Institute for Leadership, Innovation, and Excellence in Teaching at McMaster University. Alise received bachelor's degrees in English and Social Work from McMaster, a master's in environmental studies from York University, and a doctoral degree in Social Work with a graduate diploma in gender studies and feminist research from McMaster. They are also completing a master's of health science in bioethics at the University of Toronto. Working across disciplines, Alise's teaching and research has primarily contributed to Mad(ness) Studies and Critical Disability Studies. Their work can be found in journals such as *Disability & Society*, *Teaching in Higher Education*, *Social Work Education*, *Academic Psychiatry*, and *Medical Humanities*. Alise has participated in (worked at, learned from, troubled) "partnership" across positions and contexts: service user–provider partnerships, community–university partnerships, student-staff partnerships, disabled–nondisabled partnerships, and partnerships across equity–seeking groups. While a student, Alise was involved in Mad/disabled student organizing for over a decade and is now supporting and researching this work as a staff member/instructor in partnership with disabled students.

**Elizabeth Marquis** is an associate professor in the arts and science program and the School of the Arts at McMaster University. She received an honours bachelor's in psychology and theatre & film studies from McMaster, a master's in cinema studies from New York University, and a doctoral degree in performance studies from the University of Toronto. Beth's teaching and learning research focuses primarily on student–faculty partnership, the intersections between teaching and learning and questions of equity and justice, and film and media texts as public pedagogy. She has published widely on these and other topics (often in partnership with students), and her work can be found in journals such as *Pedagogy, Culture, and Society*, *Teaching in Higher Education*, and *Discourse: Studies in the Cultural Politics of Education*. From 2015–2020, Beth served as associate director (Research) at McMaster's Paul R. MacPherson Institute for Leadership, Innovation, and Excellence in Teaching, where she codeveloped and oversaw McMaster's Student Partners Program (SPP) and served as a founding coeditor of the *International Journal for Students as Partners*.

**Alison Cook-Sather** is Mary Katharine Woodworth Professor of Education at Bryn Mawr College and director of the Teaching and Learning Institute at Bryn Mawr and Haverford Colleges. She earned her bachelor's degree in English literature from the University of California, Santa Cruz, her master's degree in English education from Stanford University, and her doctoral degree in education from the University of Pennsylvania. Alison has developed internationally recognized programs that position students as pedagogical consultants to prospective secondary teachers and to practicing college faculty members. She is founding editor of *Teaching and Learning Together in Higher Education* and founding coeditor of the *International Journal for Students as Partners*. She has published eight books and over 100 articles and book chapters and given as many keynote addresses, other invited presentations, and papers at refereed conferences on six continents.

**Leslie Patricia Luqueño** is a doctoral student at Stanford University's Graduate School of Education, where she specializes in the sociology of education. Prior to her doctoral studies, the Bell Gardens, California resident graduated from Haverford College with a bachelor's degree in anthropology and educational studies in 2020. Leslie's current research focuses on the experiences of second-generation Latinx immigrant college students and the unique pockets of familial and experiential knowledge they carry that help them survive and thrive within higher education. During her time at Haverford College, she participated as a student partner with two faculty members through Bryn Mawr College's Teaching and Learning Institute. She is a coauthor of the book chapter "Valuing Knowledge(s) and Cultivating Confidence: Contributions of Student–Faculty Pedagogical Partnerships to Epistemic Justice" and her undergraduate work has earned international accolades in legal studies and sociology from *The Global Undergraduate Awards*.

*Teaching and Learning books from Stylus*

**Infusing Critical Thinking Into Your Course**
*A Concrete, Practical Approach*
Linda B. Nilson

**Creating Wicked Students**
*Designing Courses for a Complex World*
Paul Hanstedt

**Dynamic Lecturing**
*Research-Based Strategies to Enhance Lecture Effectiveness*
Christine Harrington and Todd Zakrajsek

**Designing a Motivational Syllabus**
*Creating a Learning Path for Student Engagement*
Christine Harrington and Melissa Thomas

**Course-Based Undergraduate Research**
*Educational Equity and High-Impact Practice*
Edited by Nancy H. Hensel

**POGIL**
*An Introduction to Process Oriented Guided Inquiry Learning
for Those Who Wish to Empower Learners*
Edited by Shawn R. Simonson

## Also in *The Engaged Learning and Teaching Series*

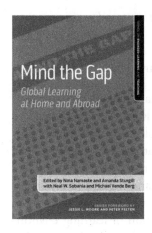

## Mind the Gap

*Global Learning at Home and Abroad*

Edited by Nina Namaste and Amanda Sturgill
With Neal W. Sobania and
Michael Vande Berg

Series Foreword by Jessie L. Moore and
Peter Felten

"This opening volume of the Elon University Center for Engaged Learning & Stylus Series on Engaged Learning & Teaching covers more than international education. The authors define 'global engagement' broadly enough to make the book a kind of master key for unlocking many High-Impact Practices, and making full use of powerful educational experiences like encounters with difference, the dissonance of unfamiliar settings, and working through ambiguity. By organizing chapters with consistent attention to context, methodology, and application, the contributors have made this an easy book to use for practitioners at a range of levels and backgrounds. What results is more than a collection of perspectives on global engagement; it's a role model for using reliable data, continuous faculty professional development, and rigorous learning outcomes assessment to tackle some of our most vexing questions."—*Ken O'Donnell, Vice Provost, California State University, Dominguez Hills*

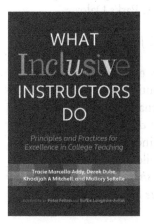

## What Inclusive Instructors Do

*Principles and Practices for Excellence in College Teaching*

Tracie Marcella Addy, Derek Dube,
Khadijah A. Mitchell, and Mallory SoRelle

This book uniquely offers the distilled wisdom of scores of instructors across ranks, disciplines and institution types, whose contributions are organized into a thematic framework that progressively introduces the reader to the key dispositions, principles and practices for creating the inclusive classroom environments (in person and online) that will help their students succeed.

## Degrees That Matter

*Moving Higher Education to a Learning Systems Paradigm*

Natasha A. Jankowski and David W. Marshall

"This book is an important reminder of the necessity for college and university actors to become aware of the critical role they play in the construction of effective learning environments. The authors advocate for a renewed sense of agency where students, faculty, and administrators do not succumb to a culture of compliance. The authors not only ask for a more active and conscious participation in the construction of learning environments, but also for a more honest and public dialogue about the dynamics that work or do not work in higher education institutions. This book is required reading for educational leaders who want to construct creative, caring, and collaborative forms of learning in higher education institutions."—*Teachers College Record*

## Connected Teaching

*Relationship, Power, and Mattering in Higher Education*

Harriet L. Schwartz

Foreword by Laurent A. Parks Daloz

Afterword by Judith V. Jordan

"Harriet Schwartz has provided a welcome and much needed contribution in our current educational climate of alienation and fragmentation. As we come to understand how connections and disconnections shape the teaching and learning enterprise, we learn to be increasingly in touch with and value the risks and rewards, the delights and dilemmas that fuel our passion for the academic life."—*Gregg Wentzell, Assistant Director, Center for Teaching Excellence, Miami University and Associate Director, Lilly Conference*

# Leading Academic Change

*Vision, Strategy, Transformation*

Elaine P. Maimon

Foreword by Carol Geary Schneider

Written by a sitting college president who has presided over transformative change at a state university, this book takes on the big questions and issues of change and change management, what needs to be done and how to do it. Writing in a highly accessible style, the author recommends changes for higher education such as the reallocation of resources to support full-time faculty members in foundation-level courses, navigable pathways from community college to the university, infusion rather than proliferation of courses, and the role of state universities in countering the disappearance of the middle class. The book describes how these changes can be made, as well as why we must make them if our society is to thrive in the 21st century.

22883 Quicksilver Drive
Sterling, VA 20166-2102      Subscribe to our email alerts: www.Styluspub.com

**ELON** UNIVERSITY | CENTER FOR Engaged Learning

The Center for Engaged Learning at Elon University (www.Center ForEngagedLearning.org) brings together international leaders in higher education to develop and synthesize rigorous research on central questions about student learning. Researchers have identified high-impact educational practices such as undergraduate research, internships, service-learning, writing-intensive courses, study abroad, living-learning communities, and so on. While we know *what* these practices are, we could know much more about three essential issues:

1. *How* to do these practices well in and across contexts
2. How to *scale* these practices to many students
3. How students *integrate* their learning across multiple high impact experiences

The Center for Engaged Learning fosters investigations of these and related questions by hosting multi-institutional research and practice-based initiatives, conferences, and seminars. To date, the Center for Engaged Learning's events have focused on topics like civic engagement, mentoring undergraduate research, global learning, residential learning, capstone experiences, and preparing students for writing beyond the university.

The Center for Engaged Learning also develops open-access resources on engaged learning practices and research for faculty and educational developers. Visit www.CenterForEngagedLearning.org to access supplemental resources for books in this series as well as weekly blog posts, hundreds of videos, and introductory resource pages on specific engaged learning topics and strategies for pursuing scholarship of teaching and learning.

Jessie L. Moore
Director
jmoore28@elon.edu

Peter Felten
Executive Director
pfelten@elon.edu